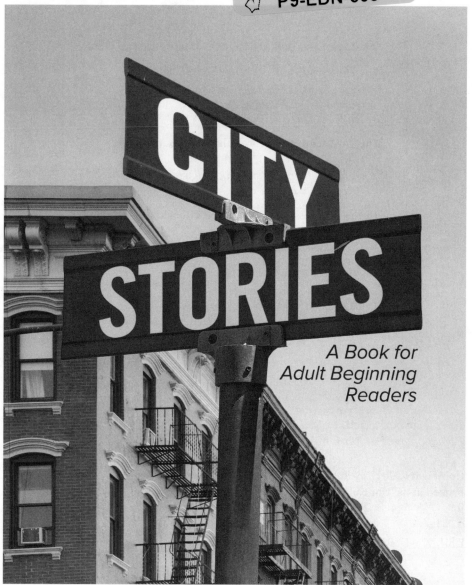

CITY STORIES

*A Book for
Adult Beginning
Readers*

LARISSA PHILLIPS

Illustrations by Christian Dechert

Other Print and Digital Resources from Townsend Press

The Townsend Press Reading Series, including:

Groundwork for College Reading with Phonics
Groundwork for College Reading
Ten Steps Plus

The Townsend Press Vocabulary Series, including:

Vocabulary Basics
Groundwork for a Better Vocabulary
Vocabulary Plus

Townsend Press Paperbacks and eBooks:

The Bluford Series
The Townsend Library

Supplements Available for *City Stories:*

Instructor's Manual and Test Bank
Companion Workbook

Cover design by Bruce Kenselaar
Text design by Janet M. Goldstein
Digital prepress by Mark Weber

Copyright © 2017 by Townsend Press, Inc.
Printed in the United States of America
9 8 7 6 5 4 3 2 1

ISBN: 978-1-59194-494-2

Send book orders and requests for desk copies to
Townsend Press Book Center
439 Kelley Drive
West Berlin, New Jersey 08091

For even faster service, contact us in any of the following ways:
By telephone: 1-800-772-6410
By fax: 1-800-225-8894
By e-mail: cs@townsendpress.com
Through our website: **www.townsendpress.com**

Contents

Introduction 1
   To the Instructor 1
   To the Student 5

Level 1: Ash Street 7
   Beth 8
   Jan 15
   Mel 22
   Pam 28
   Bill 35
   Rick 42

Level 2: Elm Street .49
   Clem 50
   Brad 59
   Ying 69
   Greg 79
   Grant 90
   Jinx 101

Level 3: Aspen Street 111
   Isad 112
   Jamal 121
   Kendrick 130
   Patrick 139
   Isabel 150
   Bethann 161

Level 4: Pine Street .177

Rose 178
James 187
June 197
Mike 206
Miles 214
Jane 225

Introduction

To the Instructor

Hello, and welcome to *City Stories!*

This book was created in response to repeated requests from my reading students. These students—so committed to their educational journey, so engaged with the mechanical aspects of decoding and encoding—would finish a lesson and ask for something to read. What an obvious and natural request this was from emerging readers! And yet I had nothing to offer them.

My searches were discouraging. Decodable reading materials were either clearly intended for children, or, if they were for adults, consisted of short passages that lacked human interest.

With no other options, I began writing the stories myself, with two essential goals in mind.

First, the text would be decodable and leveled. Instead of asking readers to simply guess the words, this text would encourage students to practice their emerging decoding skills, with each level building upon the previous level.

Second, the stories would be set in a world familiar to the adult student. Relating personally to a story can both increase students' comprehension skills and sharpen their desire to read more. Additionally, finding one's own experiences or feelings in a story makes a fundamental point: *You matter. Your stories are worthy of record. Look, here they are, in print.*

In keeping with these goals, these stories use decodable language to tell short, hopeful stories about adults with adult concerns—everything from defiant teenagers to delayed educational goals to fractured family relationships. Many of the adults in the stories are immigrants, with needs and pressures specific to the immigrant family. It is with great respect, admiration, and humility that I have borrowed experiences from the many stories my students have told me through the years to create new stories, which I hope capture some of the intensity and optimism of the originals.

At its most basic level, this collection can be used like any book: for reading. Students can take the stories home and work through them on their own. But a much more satisfying and productive experience can be achieved by incorporating the book into a reading program.

The most effective reading programs offer instruction that is multi-sensory, explicit, systematic, and cumulative. Samuel Orton and Anna Gillingham proposed such a program back in the 1930s, and the Orton-Gillingham approach remains the gold standard for teaching reading. The National Reading Panel confirmed its efficacy (at least for children) in 2000. While it can be time-consuming and require much much of both student and teacher, it is the best approach we have.

This type of instruction is **multi-sensory**, in that it takes advantage of the natural way that we all learn—mostly through sight, sound and movement. It is especially important to incorporate kinesthetic or tactile learning. In most programs, students physically manipulate letter tiles; they use gross motor movements to aid in memory retention; and when they sound out a word, they use a hand or finger motion to indicate each sound.

The instruction is **explicit**, rather than intuitive. The program will clearly teach and re-teach each rule involved in the reading process. Students learn to rely on the rules, and to trust the process of sounding out and blending. Many of my non-reading students start the program with little or no awareness of the reading process. They can't understand why they haven't been able to memorize all the words. The knowledge of the rules involved in the reading process, and the ability to put these rules to use, is a new development in these students' lifelong efforts to learn to read.

Finally, the program should be **systematic** and **cumulative**. The most basic elements are introduced first, with systematic progression as each element is mastered. There is ongoing review of mastered concepts.

In keeping with this proven approach, the stories in this book are divided into levels. Each level cumulatively builds on the previous levels so the student can continue to practice with the earlier concepts, while working toward mastery of the new concepts. The levels are as follows:

Level 1—Short vowels in words that have three sounds, such as *hat*, *shop*, and *kiss*.

Level 2—Words with consonant blends, such as *gift*, *plan*, and *bank*.

Level 3—Multi-syllabic words, such as *admit*, *finish*, and *fantastic*.

Level 4—Words with long vowels made from the vowel-consonant-*e* construction, such as *fine*, *made*, and *save*. This level also offers multi-syllabic words that contain both long and short vowels, such as *admire* and *extreme*.

Ideally, *City Stories* will be used with this type of proven reading program. Much of the language in these stories is decodable and controlled. Sight words are still used, of course; and the controlled text sometimes varies for the sake of telling a good story. To help with these departures, the *Instructor's Manual* lists the sight words, vocabulary words, and idiomatic expressions used in each story. The instructor can prep the student with these words prior to reading, or make them part of a structured reading program.

The *Instructor's Manual* provides a basic reading comprehension lesson plan that can be used with each story, including pre-reading prep, discussion questions, and exercises to be completed after reading the text.

Finally, a companion workbook is available on the Townsend Press website, **http://www.townsendpress.com**. It offers practice with sight words, prompts for reading comprehension and writing, and word games related to the text. At no charge, you can download this workbook for your students.

Attaining fluency as an adult is an enormously difficult task. It requires vast reserves of belief and determination from the student— and from the instructor as well. I applaud your efforts in supporting this most under-served population, and I encourage you to look at every small gain as a tremendous win. Even the tiniest steps make a significant impact on a student's life.

— **Larissa Phillips**

To the Student

Hello, and welcome to *City Stories!* This book was created for adult students who are learning to read and who want stories so they can practice reading.

It is not unusual for adults to have trouble reading. In the United States alone, there are 42 million adults who cannot read. If you ever feel lonely in your struggles with reading, please know that you are most definitely *not* alone.

The best way to learn to read is to be part of a reading program that has been proven to work. If you have both a good teacher and a good program, and you are committed to working hard, you will make progress.

Every step you take in your journey to become a better reader will have an impact. I have seen students improve their reading abilities to the point that they are able to

- manage their own bills
- take on-line tests in order to apply for a new job
- get around on public transportation more easily
- feel confident at work with checklists and written messages from their employers
- fill out reports at work
- read to their children or grandchildren
- do well on tests so they can get into new classes
- enter job training programs
- take computer classes
- and so much more!

How This Book Works

City Stories is divided into four levels. The stories in the first level are mostly told with very simple words. These words have short vowels and three sounds in them. These are words like *job* and *hat* and *shop*. I hope that you practice sounding out these words, rather than memorizing them. It is this ability to blend sounds into words that makes a fluent reader.

The second level still uses words with short vowels, but adds consonant blends: words like *test*, *ring*, and *gift*. The third level uses multi-syllable words, like *admit*, *finish*, and *basketball*. And the fourth level adds words with long vowels, like *mile* and *cake* and *admire*.

Sight Words, Vocabulary, and Expressions

In addition to the words that can be sounded out, there are many sight words. These are commonly used words such as *the*, *who*, and *should* that have unusual or advanced spelling rules. Teachers generally ask students to memorize these words. Your instructor can also go over any expressions or vocabulary words used in the story.

Ideally, before beginning to read each story, you should make sure you are familiar with the sight words used in that story, and that you understand and are comfortable with any expressions or special vocabulary words. You will then be ready to begin reading the story. You may want to read the story several times to get the experience of reading fluently.

After you've read the story, your instructor will probably give you worksheets. These worksheets have exercises to help you further improve your reading ability.

With a strong mind and a determined will—and a great teacher using a proven program —you can work on these stories and improve your reading. Remember that it is in your power. I so respect your determination and desire. And I wish you the success you deserve.

— **Larissa Phillips**

Level 1
Ash Street

The Men and Women of Ash Street

Beth — a gal in a shop
Jan — a mom with kids, and a good job
Mel — a man who is mad at his dad
Pam — a mom with a big shot kid
Bill — a son with no job
Rick—a man with a bad job and a big wish

Beth

Chapter One

This is Beth.
Beth is a gal.
Beth is a gal that has a lot of fun.

Beth has a job.
The job is in a shop.
It is a hat shop.

Beth is not a mom.
When Beth was a kid, Beth was the big kid.
Beth was the big kid, of six kids.

As the big kid, Beth had to get the kids fed.
She had to pick up the mess.
She had to yell at the kids.

Beth got sick of the mess.
Beth got sick of the fuss.
Beth got sick of kids!

Now Beth is big.
Beth has no kids.
She has no mess to pick up.

Beth's mom tells Beth this is not OK.
"You can not be happy with no kids."
Beth says, "Mom, I am VERY happy with no kids!"

Beth has a lot of cash.
Beth has a lot of men.
Beth has a lot of fun!

Chapter Two

There is a new hat in the hat shop.
It is a black hat. It is so fab. It is hot.
Beth has to have this hat!

Beth is all set to get this hat.
But she has to get to the doctor.
Beth has a bad back.

At the doctor's, Beth chats with a man.
The man is Ted.
Ted has a bad back, too.

Beth and Ted have a chat at the doctor's.
Ted is a good man.
Ted and Beth have a chat about their bad backs.

Ted says, "Let's chat at that hot dog shop.
We can get a hot dog and a Coke."
Beth says, "Yes!"

Ted and Beth go to the shop.
They have hot dogs. And a Coke. And a chat.
It is fun!

Then Ted says, "Um . . ."
Beth says, "Yes?"
Ted says, "Um . . ."
At last, Ted says, "Can we go to lunch on Sunday?"
Beth says, "Yes!"

Beth says, "I will put on my big black hat at the lunch."
Ted says, "OK."
Beth says, "You will love this hat!"

Chapter Three

Ted and Beth will go to lunch today.
But Beth is having a bit of a fit.
She did not get the hat yet.
The hat is still at the shop!

Beth has a big fit.
Sunday lunch with no hat?
Beth says, "OH MY GOD!
I can not go to lunch with no HAT!"

Beth runs to the car.
She is in a rush to get to the shop.
She has to get that hat!

Beth's boss is at the shop.
He says, "Hi Beth, why are you at the shop?"
Beth says, "I have to get that black hat!"

Her boss says, "The black hat?
Oh yes, that is a fab hat!
But a man just got that black hat."

Beth is all set to have a fit! She calls her pal, Jan.
"How can I go for lunch with no hat?!"
Jan says, "Beth, it is OK. Sunday lunch with no hat is OK."

Beth has no hat at lunch.
But Ted is not upset.
Ted says, "Hat? What hat?"

Ted and Beth have lunch.
Beth does not miss the hat.
Ted does not miss the hat.
Ted and Beth have a lot of fun.

Chapter Four

Beth will not be stuck with one man.
That man she had lunch with? Ted?
Ted did not last.
Beth had a chat with Ted, and she had lunch with Ted.
But that was it.

Beth's mom says,
"Beth! When will you pick a man?

When will you be a mom?
When will you stop this stuff? When?!"
Beth says, "Mom, I will not pick a man, and I will not be a mom.
I will have fun, and that is all. Fun, fun, fun!"

Beth is at the job.
Her job is at the shop in the mall that sells hats.
A man is in the shop.
"Hi," says Beth. "Can I get you a hat?"
The man will not look up.

This man is odd.
He does not pick up a hat.
He does not look at the hats.
He will not look at Beth.
It is very odd.

"Hi," says Beth. "Can I help you?"
Then Beth yells! The man has a gun!
He is not in the shop to get a hat.
He is a thug.
He is in the shop to get cash!

"Get me all the cash," the man says.
"Do not yell. Put all the cash in the box."
Beth is not OK with this!
What if this man is nuts?
What if this man kills her?!

Beth gets the cash box.
"Get me the cash!" says the man.
He has a bag. "Put the cash in the bag!"
Beth puts the cash in the bag.

Will the cops get to Beth?
Will the cops get the man?
Is the man a nut?
Will the man kill Beth?

Get to the end of Level 1 to find out!

Jan

Chapter One

This is Jan.
Jan is a mom.
Jan is from Jamaica.

When Jan was a kid, Jan was in Jamaica.
It was Jan and Mom and Jan's Gran-Gran, in Jamaica.
Jan had a dad, as well, but he was in the USA.

Jan was sad.
She was with her Gran-Gran a lot, but she did miss her Dad.
Dad did miss Jan and Mom, as well.

When Jan was ten, Jan's Mom said, "Dad has a good job,
    and he has put a lot of cash into the bank.
He says we can go to the US."
So Jan said good-bye to Gran-Gran, and got on a jet with Mom.

Jan's Dad met them at the jet.
The chill in the air was bad!
Jan had to fuss, as the chill was bad.

Mom said, "Hush, Jan. Yes, the chill is bad, but Dad has a hat."
Dad said, "Get this stuff on! Get this hat on! Zip up!"
Jan did as he said. Then the chill was not so bad.

Then, Jan was in New York City!
The city was big.
Jan was with Mom and Dad.

When Jan got big, she met Mel.
Mel and Jan fell in love.
They had kids, Sal and Pat.
They got a house on Ash Street.

Chapter Two

Jan has Mel and Sal and Pat.
Jan has a good life.
She has good kids and a good man, and she has a good job.
It is all good. Jan is all set.

But Jan has a wish.
Back when she was ten, and Jan got on that jet,
    she said good-bye to her Gran-Gran.
Gran-Gran is back home in Jamaica. She is 94!
Jan does miss her Gran-Gran.

"When will I get to see my Gran-Gran?" says Jan.
Soon it will be Gran-Gran's birthday.
Gran-Gran will be 95!
Jan has a big wish—to get back to Jamaica
    for Gran-Gran's birthday.

But Jan has no cash to get on the jet.
She can not get back to her Gran-Gran.
This is sad for Jan.
How can she miss Gran-Gran's birthday?

"Mom is sad," says Pat.
"Can we help her?" says Sal.
"Let's get the cash for Mom," says Pat.
"Then she can get on the jet, and see her Gran-Gran."

"How can we get that much cash?" says Sal.
Sal is the big kid.
She gets it that it is a lot of cash.
"We can have a tag sale," says Pat.
Pat is the small kid, with a lot of hope.
"We can sell our stuff.
We can sell our stuff to get cash for Mom."

For a tag sale, you get all your stuff that you do not want.
Pots and pans. Clothing. Dolls. Fishing rods. Toys.
Then, you make signs. "Tag Sale. Sunday. 10–2."
You sell all your stuff.

Sal and Pat had the tag sale.
It was a good day with a lot of sun.
All the people were out on Ash Street.
Sal and Pat got lots of cash for the stuff.

Chapter Three

"Mom, we got cash for you! To go see your Gran-Gran!"
Sal and Pat were so happy to tell this to Jan.
It was not a lot of cash. It was $55.
But Jan was glad.

The girls got a big hug.
"Thank you, Sal and Pat," Jan said. "Thank you!"
Jan still has to get $550. Can she get the cash?
Will she get the cash to see her Gran-Gran?"

At the job, Jan's boss saw that Jan was sad.
She said, "Jan, what is up? Are you sad?"
Jan said, "Yes, I am very sad.
My Gran-Gran will be 95 this fall.
She will have a big birthday bash, and I will miss it."

Jan said, "I miss my Gran-Gran so much.
She was a mom to me when I was a kid.
My mom was at the job a lot.
My Gran-Gran was the mom for us.
And I will not get to see Gran-Gran when she is 95."

Jan's boss said, "Jan, do not get upset.
A man quit his job with us.
You can have the shift that he had.
It is the Sunday shift.
You will get a lot of cash for the Sunday shift.
Then you can get the cash for the jet."

Jan said, "Oh! I think I can do that!
Let me check with Mel and the kids.
But I think I can do that.
Then I will get the cash for the jet, and I will get to see
    my Gran-Gran!"

What is this? Jan is on the jet!
Jan is on the jet to go see her Gran-Gran!
At the job, Jan did the Sunday shift. Soon, Jan had the cash.
Jan will see her Gran-Gran.

Jan will miss the kids.
She will miss Mel.
But it is OK.
She will get to see her Gran-Gran.

Chapter Four

Jan gets off the jet in Jamaica.
It is hot in Jamaica!
There is no chill in Jamaica.
Jan has to get rid of the hat.
This is all good.

A gal says, "Is that Jan?"
It is Kim.
Kim!
When Jan was a kid, Kim was her best pal.
Kim is at the jet to pick up Jan.

Kim says, "Jan! What is up?!"
Jan says, "It is HOT in Jamaica.
But it is so good.
I did miss all of this.
I am so glad to be back."

Kim and Jan go to Gran-Gran's.
Jan says, "Gran-Gran?"
But Gran-Gran is not there.
Where is Gran-Gran?

Kim says, "Jan!
Gran-Gran is here."
Gran-Gran is in bed.
Is Gran-Gran sick?
No, Gran-Gran is OK.

Jan says, "Gran-Gran?"
Gran-Gran says, "Jan? My baby gal?"
Jan says, "I am big, but I am Jan."
Gran-Gran says, "Baby gal! I did miss my baby gal!"
At last, Jan gets to hug her Gran-Gran.

Jan was there for Gran-Gran's big birthday bash.
Jan got to see all her pals from when she was a kid.
Jan's Gran-Gran would not quit with the hugs for Jan.
"It is so good to be with my gal," says Jan's Gran-Gran.
"I missed my Jan."

Jan calls Mel and the kids.
"It is so good to be here," she says.
"I am glad to see all my pals,
    and my Gran-Gran.
But I miss you all, too.
Next time, let's all go!"

Mel

Chapter One

This is Mel.
Mel is the dad of Sal and Pat.
Mel is Jan's husband.

Mel has a job in a shop.
It is a good job.

When Mel was a kid,
    Mel's dad was mad a lot.
His dad would yell a lot.
His dad hit Mel a lot.

Mel said, "When I am big, I will NOT get mad at the kids.
I will NOT hit my kids.
I will NOT yell at my kids."

Now Mel is a dad.
Mel has good kids.
But . . . kids will be kids.

Sal and Pat will fuss.
Sal and Pat will mess stuff up.
Sal will yell at Pat, and Pat will yell back at Sal.

When his kids get mad, Mel will get a bit mad.
But he will not hit his kids.
He will not yell back at his kids.

Mel hugs his kids a lot.
And his kids will hug and kiss him back.
Mel is a good dad, and a good man.

Chapter Two

Mel is big now.
He does not yell, or hit his kids.
He will not be like his dad.

But Mel is still mad at his dad.
He will not chat with his dad.
And he will not see him.

But now Mel's dad is sick.
Mel's dad calls Mel.
Mel will not pick up the call.

Mel has a sis, Deb.
Deb is not mad at their dad.
Deb says, "Mel, Dad is sad that you will not see him."

Deb says, "Mel, Dad calls for you.
You have to see him."
Mel says to Deb, "Dad can go to hell."

Deb says, "Mel! Dad is sick!
Soon Dad will not be with us.
He is very sick."

Mel says, "So what?
Dad hit me when I was a kid.
He was such a bad dad."

Now Deb is mad at Mel.
And Mel is mad at their dad.
And their dad is still very sick.

Chapter Three

Deb will not stop.
"Mel! Dad is sick.
A son has to go to his dad.
A son has to check on his dad."

Mel is still mad at his dad.
But he is sad that his dad is sick.
What if his dad will not get well?
What if this is it?

Mel thinks back to when he was a kid.
When he was a kid, his dad did yell.
And he did hit him.
But he was still a dad.

His dad would say, "Mel, get the fishing rod.
Let's go fishing."
And they would go fishing all day.
Mel and his dad got lots of fish.

And if a kid was bad to Mel, his dad got mad.
His dad would say, "Mel is my kid.
Do not mess with my kid!"
Mel's dad was not all bad.

Mel thinks of all this.
He thinks of when his dad
    did good stuff.
He thinks of when his dad
    was a good dad.
He thinks of his dad in bed,
    sick and old.

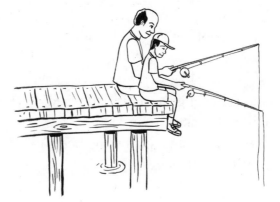

But Mel is still mad.
It is not OK that his dad hit him.
He can't let go of this.
But . . . his dad is sick.

At last, Mel says, "I will go to my dad."
He calls Deb to tell her.
Deb says, "Oh good, Mel!
Dad will be so happy to see you."

Chapter Four

Mel is on his way to see his dad.
Will his dad be mad at him?
Will he still hit Mel?
And yell at him?

Mel is not at all himself.
He gets lost in the halls of the hospital.
His hands are wet.
He can not get a good breath.

At last, Mel gets to his dad's bed.
His dad is asleep.
Mel goes in and sits by the bed.
Mel's dad sleeps.

Mel has not seen his dad in 15 years.
His dad is now an old man.
His dad is not big and bad.
He is small and old.

"Mel?" It is Mel's dad.
"Mel, is that you?"
His dad is old and sick, in bed.
He is so sick.

"Hi, Dad. It is me. It is Mel."
"Mel! I am so glad to see you,"
    says Mel's dad.
He picks up Mel's hand.
"I am glad to see you, too, Dad," says Mel.

After that, Mel goes to see his dad a lot.
Mel's dad wants to tell him something.
"Mel," he says, "I was not a good dad.
I can see that. And I am sorry, Mel."

"It's OK, Dad," says Mel. "There was good stuff, too."
"Like the fishing?" says his dad.
"Yes, Dad, the fishing!"
"You were the best at fishing, Mel."
Mel gives his dad a hug.
He is glad he is here with his dad.

Pam

Chapter One

This is Pam.
Pam is a mom.
Pam has a job with a doctor.

Pam has a man.
Pam's man is Seth.
But Seth is still back in Chad, in Africa, with a job.

And Pam has a kid, Bill.
Bill is a big kid. He is 14.
Pam and Bill both miss Seth.

Seth will not call.
Does Seth miss Pam and Bill?
Will Seth get to the US? When?

Bill is 14.
Uh oh!
Bill is not a man yet, but he is a big shot.

Bill is a big, *big* shot.
Bill says, "Mom, I am a big man.
I am a hot shot."

Bill is hot stuff.
Bill's dad is not in the US.
Pam has to be the mom and the dad.

Chapter Two

Bill sits on his butt all day.
He chats with pals, and plays on his phone.
This gets Pam so mad.
She says, "That kid will not do what he has to do!"

Pam has a pal, Beth.
(Beth is the gal that has the job in the hat shop.)
Pam says to Beth, "What do I do with Bill?
He is not a big man. He is a kid."

Pam tells Beth, "He will not get the stuff at the shop.
He will not shut the shed.
He will not pick up his mess.
I have had it with him."

Beth is chill.
She says, "Pam, it is OK. He is 14.
Yes, he is a big shot.
But that is how kids are."

Beth says, "When he is a man, he will get it.
Do not get upset with him.
Just let him be."
But Pam is upset with this kid.

Pam says to Bill, "Bill, get the stuff at the shop.
Shut the shed.
Pick up the mess."
Pam says, "Bill, if you do not do this, I will get very mad."

Bill says, "Mom, you do not get it.
I am a big shot. I am a big bad man.
I do not get stuff or pick up the mess.
I am hot stuff."

Pam is fed up. She calls Seth.

"When can you get to the US?" she says.

"Bill has to have a dad. I can not do this by myself."

"I will finish the job soon," Seth says.

"Then I will get to the US."

Chapter Three

Pam has a boss, Dr. Smith.

Pam says to Dr. Smith, "I am so upset with my kid.

Back in Chad this would not be OK.

When I was a kid, I did not do this stuff."

Pam's boss, Dr. Smith, is not upset.

"Pam, this is the US," he says.

"This is what the kids are like in the US.

He is a US kid. Do not get upset with him."

But Pam is not OK with this.

She says to Beth, "I can not bring up this kid by myself.

I am at the job all day.

I can not check on him all the time."

Pam has had it.

She is mad.

She is fed up with this kid!

She has a fit.

Pam says to Bill, "Bill, GET UP!
Get OFF the bed.
Shut OFF the TV.
Pick UP the mess."

Bill says, "Get off my back, Mom!
I am a big bad man, and I am hot stuff.
I am not your DOG!"
Uh oh. This is bad.

Pam says to Bill, "THAT IS IT!
You will not get cash from me!
YOU get the bill for the cell phone!
No cash! You get no cash from me!"

Pam runs out.
Bill is by himself.
No cell phone? No cash?
What?!!

Chapter Four

Pam has cut off Bill.
No cash. No cell phone.
Bill is so upset.
He did not think his mom would get so mad.

This is big for Bill.
He is not a big shot with no cash and no cell phone.
He is not a big man.
He is just a kid.

And his mom is so mad at him.
She will not chat with him.
She will not fix his dinner for him.
She will not sit with him.

OK, so then he will not sit with her.
He will not chat with his mom.
He will let her see how mad he is.
A 14-year old can be very mad.

Pam and Bill are in a mess.
Then—Pam gets a call.
It is Seth.
Seth is her man, who is at his job in Chad.

"Pam! It is Seth!"
Pam says, "Seth? Is that you?"
Seth says, "Yes, Pam. It is me, Seth.
I have big news.
My job is all done.
I will come to the US."

Pam says, "What? You will come to the US? When?"
Seth says, "I have to get my visa.
Then I will come to the US.
It should be in six weeks."

Pam says, "WOW!
Seth, that is good news."
She looks at Bill, who will not chat with her.
"Seth, we need you here."

Bill

Chapter One

Bill's mom is so mad at him.
She has cut him off.
She says he is not a big man,
    and not a big shot.
She says he should pick up the
    mess, get stuff at the shop,
    and get OFF his butt!

Bill is sick of this.
No cash, no cell phone, no girls.
And his mom is so mad at him.
He sees his mom's pal, Beth.
"What's up, Bill?" says Beth. "You look sad."
"I am not sad, I am *mad*," says Bill.
"My mom cut me off."

"You can not get cash from her? So? Get a job," says Beth.
"What? A job?" says Bill. "But I am just a kid."
"What?" says Beth. "But you said you were a big man!"
"Well, yes, but . . . no. I can't get a job!"

Beth says, "You can get a job.
Lots of shops will pay you.
It will not be much.
But it will be a job.
You will have cash.
Then you will be more like a man."

"Hmm," says Bill.
"A job. Yes, a job!
I will get a job!"
He goes to the shops on Ash Street.
But it is hard to go into the shops.

What if they say no?
What if they think he is just a kid?
It will be so bad if they say no to him!
What will he do?

In the end, he goes into a rug shop.
"Hi, I want a job," he says to the man.
"Do you need a kid to do stuff in this shop?
I can do lots of stuff."

"No," says the man. "No jobs in this shop."
This "no" did not kill Bill!
He goes to a lot of shops to get a job.
At last, he gets a job. It is at a pet shop.

Chapter Two

Bill has a job!
At the job, he has to do a lot of stuff.
He has to pick up the mess.
He has to get stuff for the dogs and cats.

He has to put stuff on the shelf.
The boss tells him what to do.
And then he has to do it.
It is not big stuff, but he does it.

But it is fun to be a kid with a job!
Bill's pals come into the shop to say hi.
"Get out of here," Bill says.
"I have lots of stuff to do."

He is a big hot shot with a job!
He gets a pay check.
It is not a big check.
But it is a check, and he can cash it.

Now Bill has cash!
When he is with his pals,
    he is the kid with the cash.
He can get the check.
He can tell the girls,
    "Let me get that for you."

This is so good for Bill!
He is good at his job.
He gets it that he has to pick up the mess.
He has to do the stuff that the boss wants him to do.

Bill goes back to his mom.
"Mom," he says, "I get it.
I will get stuff at the shop for you.
I will pick up the mess.
I will do what you want me to do."

Bill gets a kiss and hug from his mom.
Pam says with a grin, "Bill, you are a hot shot!"
Then she says, "And Dad will be here soon!
He will be glad to see you have a job."

Chapter Three

Pam and Bill are at the airport.
They can see the jet.
Seth is on that jet.
Bill has not seen his dad in six years. Six years!
Will this be bad? Will it be hard?
What will this be like?

Bill and his mom can see Seth.
Here he is!
Big hug.

Seth says, "Bill! You are a big man!"
Bill says, "Yes, I am. See, Mom? I am a big man."

Pam says, "Seth, you should see him at his job.
He is a big kid, with a job in a shop."
"You have a job?" says Seth to Bill. "YOU?"
But Bill will not tell his dad about his job.

Bill's job is so small.
He wants his dad to see him in a big job.
Not this small job where he picks up dog mess.
Not this job where he has to do what his boss tells him to do.

Bill runs out to go to his job.
He will not tell his dad that he has to go to his job.
"Bill!" his dad calls.
He runs after him.

Seth goes into the pet shop.
Bill is there.
Seth sees him pick up the mess.
He puts stuff on the shelf.

"Dad!" Bill is in shock to see his dad.
"Why are you here?"
He acts like he is mad to see his dad.
But he is just sad that he does not
    have a big job.

Seth is so proud to see Bill at his job.
"Bill!" he says. "You are a big kid.
You should not be sad about this.
This is a good job for a kid!"

Chapter Four

At home, Bill's dad is in the way.
He has no job yet. He has nothing to do.
Back in Chad, he was a big man on the job.
Now he is just in the way.
Bill and Pam have jobs and lots of stuff to do.

Seth sits at home.
He will not look for a job.
He is in bed all day.
He will not go out.

"Did you get a job?" Pam says when she gets back.
"Uh," says Seth.
"Yes or no?" says Pam.
"Well, uh, no."

Pam is fed up with Seth.
"You just sit on your butt all day!" she yells.
"I am at my job and then I shop for food.
Then I get home and I do dinner.
You? You do nothing!"

Seth gets mad.
"I got to the US one month ago!
I get to chill for a bit!
Bill, back me up!
Tell your mom I get to chill."

Bill has to get to his job.
But he says, "Mom, Dad gets to chill for a bit.
It's hard to get to the US.
When we got here, it was hard.
Let's let Dad chill for a bit."

Then Bill says, "But Dad? You can get a job.
Lots of shops will pay you.
It will not be much. But it will be a job.
You will have cash. You can do it.
And we will be proud of you."

Seth has to grin.
"Look at this kid,"
    says Seth.
"You did a good job
    with him, Pam."
Pam grins back at Seth.
Bill runs out to his job,
    with a big grin, too.

Rick

Chapter One

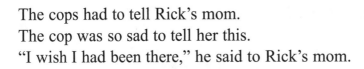

This is Rick.
Rick is a young man. He is 21.
When Rick was a kid, he was in Trinidad.

Back in Trinidad, when Rick was 13,
    his dad was killed.
A man tried to rob his dad.
His dad did not let the man have his cash, and the man killed him.

The cops had to tell Rick's mom.
The cop was so sad to tell her this.
"I wish I had been there," he said to Rick's mom.

The cop had his hat off.
He had so much to say to Rick's mom.
But he just said "I'm sorry," again and again.

Rick and his mom were in shock.
"How can this be?" his mom said, through her sobs.
"How can we go on?"

It was bad enough to miss Rick's dad so much.
But now, they also had no cash.
Rick's mom could not get a job.

With no cash for rent, they had to stay with a pal of Rick's mom.
Rick and his mom had no bed.
This was not good, and there were still no jobs.

Rick's mom had a sis in New York City.
Rick's mom sat him down and said,
    "Rick, my sis says she can get me a job."
Rick said to his mom, "Let's go!"

Chapter Two

Rick and his mom took a jet to New York City.
Rick's mom got a job.
She works a lot, but she is happy to have a job.
Rick went to high school in New York.

Now Rick is big, and out of school.
His mom says, "Rick, you should go to college."
But Rick is so sick of being a kid.
He wants to help his mom out.

Rick wants a job now!
So he does not go back to school.
He gets a job in a shop.
This is good. He can help his mom.

His job is in the back of a shop.
Rick has to mop the shop, and he has to pick up the mess.
He gets to the job at 6 AM.
He is at the job until 8 PM.
If Rick is at all late, the boss yells at him.

The boss is mad at Rick a lot.
He yells at Rick.
"What the hell, kid? Pick that up!"
Rick has to run and pick it up.

The boss has a big dog.
The dog sits in the back of the shop.
Rick can tell that this is a bad dog.
That dog is all set to get Rick.

Rick does not like this job at all.
He says to his mom, "I have to get a new job.
The boss is bad, the dog is bad, and the job is bad."
Rick's mom says, "Well, then, get a new job."

Rick says, "Mom, I want to be a cop.
If I am a cop, I can get bad men. Like the one that got Dad."

Rick's mom says, "OK, get a job as a cop.
You can get that job!"

Chapter Three

Rick goes to chat with his pal, Mel.
(Mel is the man with the sick dad.)
Mel knows that Rick has no dad.
He is like a dad to Rick.
Rick says, "Mel, what do I do?
My wish is to be a cop."

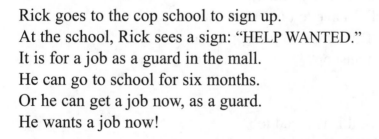

Mel says, "Rick, this is what you do.
There is a school for cops.
You sign up at the school.
You do the work. You pass the test.
And then you get to be a cop."
Rick says, "Is that all? OK, I can do that!"

Rick goes to the cop school to sign up.
At the school, Rick sees a sign: "HELP WANTED."
It is for a job as a guard in the mall.
He can go to school for six months.
Or he can get a job now, as a guard.
He wants a job now!

Rick calls. "Hi, this is Rick. I am calling for the job.
The job for a guard in the mall."

"Can you come in for a chat with the boss?"
Rick says, "Yes!"
Rick chats with the boss. He gets the job!

Rick goes to tell Mel.
Mel is like a dad to him.
"I got a job! I do not need to go to school!
I got a job as a guard in the mall.
That is all I need. No school for me."

Mel says to Rick, "A job is good.
But you will not get as much for that job as you would
    if you are a cop."
Rick says, "But I will look like a cop. I will look so cool!"
Mel says, "Rick, get this job, but you should go to school as well."
Rick says, "No, this job is good. It is all I need."

Rick tells his boss that he has to quit.
His boss says, "What? No, Rick, you can not do that.
I can not run this shop if you quit."
Rick says, "Well, I have to quit. I have a new job."
His boss says, "But who will pick up the mess
    and mop up the shop?"

Rick says, "Boss, this is a bad job.
The cash is bad, the mess is bad, and the dog is bad.
And the boss is bad.
I quit!
Good-bye!"

Chapter Four

Rick is at his new job at the mall.
Rick has a cool hat. He looks like a cop.
But he is not a cop.
His job is not a big job.
He can not get bad men.
It is a small job. And it is very dull.

There is not a lot for him to do at the mall.
He checks out all the shops.
He chats with the moms.
He tells the kids not to yell.
He tells the kids not to push.
The job is very dull.

The best part of his job is the gal in the hat shop.
She is so cute!
When he gets to pass the hat shop,
     he says hi.
He stops and chats with her.
She tells him her name is Beth.

One day he gets up to the hat shop.
He can see Beth.
But she does not look OK.
She looks odd.
Then he sees why.

There is a man in the shop.
A man with a gun! It is a thug.
The thug has the gun out as he gets the cash from Beth.
Beth sees Rick but does not say a thing.
Rick has to do something!

First, he puts in a call for back-up. "Get to the hat shop, quick!"
Then he goes to the shop and gets down by the door.
He sits there.
When the thug with the gun comes out, Rick gets up quick.
He grabs the thug and gets him to fall down.
He grabs the gun.

When his back-up gets to the hat shop, Rick has the man.
Rick is happy.
Beth is happy.
"Thank you, Rick! You are the best cop!"
Rick does not tell Beth that he is not a cop.
Why should he? He did the job of a cop, didn't he?

Rick says to Beth, "Can I call you?
We can get a drink. And . . . there is something I should tell you."
Rick is all set to tell Beth that he is not a cop.
Beth says, "Yes sir, Mr. Cop!"
And then she gives him a kiss.
So, maybe he will tell her later.

Will Rick tell Beth that he is not a cop?
Get to the end of Level 4 to find out!

Level 2
Elm Street

The Men and Women of Elm Street

Clem — a mom who brags too much
Brad — a man who left the drug wars and must get a job
Ying — a woman from Hong Kong who must learn English
Greg — a man who got to the US in the hold of a ship
Grant — a man whose wife will have twins
Jinx — a woman from the Bronx who wants a ring

Clem

Chapter One

This is Clem.
Clem has two sons.
Clem's sons are good in school.
Clem brags to all her pals.

Clem's sons get all A's in school.
On the job, Clem says, "Check this out!
My kids are the best kids.
My kids get the best marks."

Clem says, "Trev is the best at math.
Trev gets all A's on his math tests.
Fred is the best at English.
Fred gets all A's on his English tests."

Clem's pal are sick of this.
When Clem is not at the job, they say, "I am so sick of Clem!
Clem has got to stop.
She brags too much!"

But Clem will not stop.
She says, "My boys are the best.

They get gold stars and all A's in English.
They win gold medals."

Clem holds up the test.
She holds it up, but something is off.
She holds the test wrong.
And it is not an English test.

Clem's pal Fran says,
"Hmm. This is not right.
Clem holds up the test wrong.
And she says it is an English test, but it is not."

Clem's pal Fran says, "I do not think Clem can read."
Fran has a plan. It is kind of a bad plan.
She says, "I will set a trap for Clem.
I will trick Clem to show us all that she can not read."

Chapter Two

Clem is at the job.
Clem says, "Look, Fran.
My kids got the best marks in the class on this test."
Fran rolls her eyes and says, "Oh yes. What a shock."
Then Fran gets a test from her bag.

Watch as Fran sets the trap for Clem!
"Clem," she says, "Can I get some help from you?
My kids did not do so well on their tests.
I must help them to do well on the next test. Can you help me?"
"What?" says Clem. "Why me?"

"Your kids get the best marks on their tests," says Fran.
"You tell us this all the time.
If you can help them get such good marks, you should help me
    and my kids."
Clem looks a bit sick.
"OK," she says at last.

Fran calls to all the men and women at the job,
    "Watch Clem help me!"
Fran says this with a wink. It is not a kind wink.
Lots of people are sick of Clem.
They think she brags too much.
They want to see her mess up.
"Let's see, Clem," they say. "Help Fran!"

Fran hands Clem the test.
All the people watch as Clem stands still and gets red.
"Get on it, Clem," says Fran. "Can you help or not?"
In her mind, Clem goes back to when she was a small kid.
She is in the front of her class.
But when the teacher calls on her, she can not read.

Back at the job, Clem is still red.
All the people look glad to see her mess up.
Fran stands next to her, with a big grin.
"OK, I can not read!" Clem yells.
Clem runs from the lunch room.
In the bathroom stall, she sobs and sobs.

Back in the lunch room, it is Fran's turn to get red.
"That was not kind, Fran," says a man.
"Fran, why did you do that?" asks a woman.
Fran feels bad. "It was just a small trick.
I did not think it would be this bad," she says.

Fran finds Clem at the sink in the bathroom.
"I'm so sorry, Clem," she says.
Clem nods. "It's OK. I should not brag so much.
But I am so proud of my kids.
I was the bad kid in school.
When I could not spell or read, the teachers hit me.
In the end, I quit school. I did not get to read."
Fran says, "I can help you. I can help you find a class."

Chapter Three

Clem has to get to her class, but she can not find it.
She thinks, *I will ask that woman for help.*
"Miss?" she says, "I can not find this class. Can you help me?"
The woman says, "Yes, this . . . my class, too!
I help you . . . get . . . class.
Clem, I am Ying. It is good class. Come."

Ying can not speak English so well.
But she has a kind face, with quick,
    kind eyes.
She asks Clem where she is from.
Clem says, "I am from Russia."
Ying is from China.
She pats Clem's hand. "We will get English!"

Clem and Ying find the class.
Ying is glad to be in class.
But for Clem, class is a bad thing.
When Clem was a kid, the teacher hit Clem.
She had to hold out her hand, and the teacher hit her hand
    with a stick.
Clem knows this teacher will not hit her, but she is still scared.

The class is a bit odd.
The teacher tells the men and women to say things.
"Hello. My name is Clem." Or, "Hello, my name is Ying."
Then they say, "Hello, Clem, how are you? I am fine."

This is OK for Clem. She is good at this!
But will this help her to read?

Then the teacher hands out a paper.
"Put your name and address on the paper," she says.
She tells the students to put lots of things on the paper.
But she still did not tell the students how to read or write.
Clem is upset.
She still can not do this.

At home, Clem gets out her book from class.
"What are you doing, Mama?" asks Clem's son Fred.
"Nothing," she says. She puts the book back in her bag.
Clem has not told her kids that she is in a class.
Clem has not told her kids that she can not read.
They know she can not read. But they do not talk about it.

At the end of the next class, the teacher wants to talk to Clem.
Clem shakes as she gets to the teacher's desk.
"Clem, this is your test. You did not do well."
Clem says, "Yes, but I will get it. I will not stop until I get it."
The teacher says, "Clem, I do not think this is the class for you."
"What?" Clem is upset. "I want to be in this class!"
"I am sorry, Clem. This is not the class for you."

Clem is so upset. The teacher wants to kick her out of class!
"What do I do if I can not be in this class?" she asks.
"It is okay, Clem," says the teacher. "This is not the end.

There is a class at the library.
The class is for men and women who can not read.
The teacher will help you to read."
"What is this class for?" asks Clem.
"This class is for men and women who want to learn English.
It is not for men and women who want to learn to read."

Chapter Four

Clem is in the new class.
The class is good!
The class is for men and women who can not read.
At last, Clem can read a bit.
But there still a thing that Clem must do.
The teacher says, "Get help at home. Get help from your kids."

Clem will not tell the kids that she can not read.
Clem's kids know. It is just a thing that they do not say.
Clem is upset that she must say this to the kids.
But she must get the help from them.
At last, Clem says, "Kids, I must ask for help from you.
I am in a class. The class is to learn to read.
And I must get help from you."
The kids nod. "Yes, Mama. That is great!"

The kids are glad that Clem is in a class.
"Mama," they say, "we think you are strong and brave.
We are so proud of you.
You are the best mom."

Clem gets a big hug from her sons.
She says, "I am proud of you kids."

Clem gets stuck at the blends.
One day she runs into her pal Ying.
"Clem!" says Ying with a grin. "How are you? I am fine!"
"I am fine, too," says Clem. "How is the English class?"
"Oh Clem," says Ying. "That class is so good.
My English is so good now! And how is the reading class?"
Clem shrugs. "Well, I am stuck. My kids help me,
    but I am still stuck."
Ying says, "Then you must ask the teacher for help."

At the end of class, Clem asks the teacher for help.
She does not want to ask, but she must.
"I can not get past the blends," she says.
The teacher does not get mad.
He wants to help.
"Can you get to a computer?"
    he asks.
"Yes," says Clem.
"My kids have a computer."
"There is a web site that can help
    you," says the teacher.

Clem gets to the web site.
She will not stop trying.
She gets past the blends.

One day, Clem is at a shop.
Fred calls on his cell. "Mama, where are you?" he says.
Clem looks up. She says, "I am at the end of Elm Street.
I am at Elm and Mink Street.
I am next to the shag rug shop.
I am past the ring shop, and next to the butcher shop.
I am at the bus stop."
Fred says, "Wow, Mama. You can read all that!"

Clem can read.
She gets a card from a pal, and she can read it.
She gets a letter from the bank, and she can read it.
She gets a card from the boss, and she can read it.
She gets the newspaper, and she can read it.
She gets a menu in the restaurant, and she can read it.
She gets a map for the bus, and she can read it.

This is the best part.
Clem is on the job. Her pal Fran is there.
"Fran, look at this. Did you see this test?
It got the best mark in the class.
It is not my kids' test. It is *my* test."
Fran and Clem grin, and Fran hugs Clem.
"Great job, Clem!"
Clem can still brag.
But now, when Clem brags, it is about Clem.

Brad

Chapter One

This is Brad.
Brad is from Guatemala.
Brad's grandpa was a big man in the town.
Brad is proud that he is the grandson
   of this man.
Brad loves his town.

In Guatemala, Brad had a job.
His job was to weld.
His job was in a shop that could weld and press metal rods.
It was a good job.
The cash was good, and Brad was proud of his job.

But in Guatemala there were drug wars.
Guatemala was in the drug path, of drugs on their way to the US.
The men who sold the drugs did not want the cash from the drugs
   to go to anyone else.
They had a war to hold on to all the cash and all the drugs.

Brad did not want to be in the drug wars.
His town had lost a lot to the drug wars.
His mom and dad did not go out of the house.
His pals had left the town.
The kids in his family did not go to school.
There was not much left, just the drugs and the war.

And so, Brad left his town.
He left his dad and his mom and all the kids.
He left the drug wars.
His plan? He will go to the US, and get a job.
He will send the cash to his mom and dad.

Brad went to New York City on a bus.
When he got to New York City, he did not have a lot of cash left.
He had to find his pal, Mark. Mark was from Guatemala, too.
Mark had told him, "You can crash with me."
Brad said, "Crash?"
Mark said, "That means you can stay at my house."

Brad did find Mark at last.
Mark was glad that Brad got to New York City.
"Come in! Come in! My friend! At last you got to the US!"
Mark said, "You must rest!"
Mark fed Brad, and let him rest.
Mark said, "If you are OK with the couch, you can be here
    as long as you want."

Mark is so glad to be in the US.
But he must find a job in a rush.
He has no green card. He has no cash.
He must get cash to help his family.
And he must get cash to help himself.
This is a lot of stress for one man.

Chapter Two

Brad is in luck. He speaks English.
His English is not the best, but it is good enough.
"Hi, I am looking for a job," he says.
"Hello, do you need help?" he asks.
"Hi, can I help?"
"Can I get a job with you?"
He asks this all day long.

Back home, Brad was a welder. Brad finds a welding shop.
"Hello, I am looking for a job. I am a welder."
The boss says, "Do you have a certificate?"
Brad says, "Certificate?"
The boss says, "Yes, you must have a certificate to get a job
    in this shop."
Brad says, "How do I get the certificate?"
The boss says, "You must pass a test."

Brad's next stop: The New York City School of Welding.
"Hello," he says. "Is there a class for welding?"
The lady says, "Yes. The next class is in two months.
The cost is $2500. It is a six-month class."
"What?" says Brad. "I must get a job now.
I can not spend months on this class. I must get cash now."
"Sorry," says the lady. "I can not help you."

Brad is sick of this. He can not find a job!
At Mark's house, he just eats rice and beans.
Brad has no cash to send to his mom and dad.

He sits on a bench and is sad.
"Hey man," a guy says.
Brad nods back at the guy.
"What's up, man? Why so glum?"
Brad shrugs. "No job, man."
"You want a job, man? I can help you."

The guy is Trent.
Trent is a guy with a lot of tricks.
Trent has lots of jobs for Brad.
He asks Brad to bring a bag to a shop, for $100.
Brad says, "What? Just bring this bag to that shop?
And I will get all that cash for that?"
Trent says, "Hey, man, just do the things I ask,
    and you will get that cash."

Brad brings the bag to that shop.
The next day, he brings a black bag to a shop on Ash Street.
And the next day he brings a pink back pack to a shop on Elm Street.
He goes to a shop to find Trent. But he does not chat with Trent.
Trent has left a bag or a back pack in the shop for Brad.
Brad gets the bag or the back pack, and goes to the shop.
And then he gets his cash from Trent.

At last, Brad has cash to spend!
He spends his cash on food.
He spends his cash on clothing.
And he gives Mark cash for rent.
But most of his cash, he sends back home to his mom and dad.
It is a thrill for Brad that he has cash, and can send it home.

The job gets big.
And then it gets bigger.
And bigger.
Trent has Brad pick up bags at all the pick-up spots.
Then Brad brings the bags to all the drop-off spots.
Trent says Brad is a big man for him.
He says he has big plans for Brad.
Brad does not check what is in the bags.
He does not want to know.

Chapter Three

Brad's job is to bring a bag or a back pack from one spot
    to another spot.
It can be a shop, or a spot in the mall, or any kind of spot.
Trent will call or text and say, "I got a pick-up."
He will tell Brad the spot for the pick-up and the spot
    for the drop-off.
Brad jumps up and runs to the job.
Trent says, "Brad, you are the man! You are the best."

Mark wants to know what job Brad has.
"Wow!" he says. "You get a lot of cash for that job."
Brad nods, but he does not say a thing.
Mark says, "What kind of job is it? Is it a welding job?"
Brad says, "No, it's not a welding job."
"So what is it?"
"It's . . . um . . . in a shop."
Brad will not tell Mark what his job is.

Brad is glad he has all this cash.
He can not think about what is in the bags.
He has a lot of cash.
His mom and dad think he has a job as a welder.
"Brad," his dad says. "Thank you.
What would we do if you did not send us this cash?"
His mom is glad, too. "Brad! You are a big man now!"
Brad's mom wants Brad to send for his sisters.
"The girls must go the US, too," she says.
"This drug war will not end. It is a mess here!
They must get to the US, and go to school.
You must help them, Brad."
Brad says, "Mama, not yet."

Brad is on the job.
He must get this bag to a spot in the mall.
It is a shop that sells hats.
He is glad to go to this drop-off spot.
The gal in the shop is a fox!
"Hey lady," he says to the gal.
"Hi hon," she says. It is Beth.
Beth is not in on the drop-off.
Brad will drop off the bag, and then he will chat with Beth,
    and maybe get a hat.

"What can I help you find?" says Beth to Brad.
"I want a hat for my sis," says Brad. "It is her birthday."
Brad puts the back pack next to a stack of hats.
Then he lets Beth help him find a hat.
A man comes in, and picks up the bag. He gets the bag and goes.

Brad checks out a lot of hats, and then picks
   a black hat with pink dots for his sis.
"Thanks!" he says to Beth.
"Thank you," says Beth with a wink.

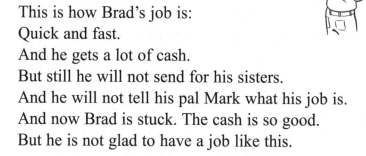

This is how Brad's job is:
Quick and fast.
And he gets a lot of cash.
But still he will not send for his sisters.
And he will not tell his pal Mark what his job is.
And now Brad is stuck. The cash is so good.
But he is not glad to have a job like this.

At Brad's next drop-off, something is off.
The drop-off spot is a rug shop.
Brad gets to the shop and goes in.
He looks for the spot that Trent told him to find, to put the bag.
"Hello, can I help you?" the rug shop man asks him.
"Yes," says Brad, "I must get a rug. A big red rug.
But I want to look at the rugs a bit."
Brad finds the spot, behind a shelf. But then—
A man is in the shop. He has a gun.
"I want that bag!" he yells.

Brad is in shock.
He did not think this was a part of this job.
But he wants to keep the bag.
He gets down behind the shelf.
BANG! BANG!
The gun goes off.

The rug man yells and yells.
"I want that bag!" the gun man yells.
The gun man gives a push to the shelf, and it falls down.
And Brad is there.
Brad puts his hands up.
"This is the bag!" he says.
The man with the gun grabs the bag.
He smacks Brad with the back end of the gun. And he runs out.

Chapter Four

Brad has a black eye and a bad cut.
Bran has to get out of this shop.
He gets up and runs.
Then he stops. He can not run.
He can not go fast.
The cops are at the rug shop.
Brad pulls his hat down.
He walks past the cops.

When Brad gets home, Mark is upset.
"What is that?" he asks.
"What is what?" Brad says.
"You got a black eye! And a big cut."
"Oh," says Brad. He has to think fast.
"I . . . I . . . I fell." He can not look Mark in the eye.
Mark can tell that this is not the truth.

Brad is in bed when Mark calls him.
"Brad, there is a guy at the door."
Brad gets up and goes to the door.
It is Trent.
"Hi man, what's up? You OK?"
"I am OK," says Brad.
"Wow! Look at that black eye!"
"Yes, it is OK."
"I am glad," says Trent. "You still up for the job?"

Brad has to ask Trent what is in the bags.
"I did not check in the bags," he says to Trent.
"But now I must know what is in them."
Trent shrugs. "Why do you want to find out?"
Brad says, "If a man could kill me for the stuff
    in the bags, I must find out.
What is in the bags?"
Trent looks Brad in the eye.
"Drugs," he says. "Drugs, and cash."

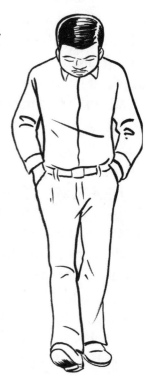

Brad is on the job.
He is still on the job for Trent.
He wants to quit.
But it is hard to let go of that much cash.
He must get cash for his mom and dad
    and for his rent.
What can he do for cash if he quits this job?
Brad has a bag. It has cash or drugs in it.
He must get the bag to the hat shop.

When Brad gets to the mall, there is a cop in the hat shop.
The cop chats with Beth, the gal who runs the hat shop.
"Hi!" says Beth to Brad.
The cop looks at Brad. He looks Brad up and down.
(It is not a cop! It is just Rick, the guard!)
Brad is upset.
He runs out of the shop and calls Trent.
"Trent? There is a cop in the shop.
I must bring this bag back to you.
Oh, and Trent? I quit."

Brad goes back to the welding shop.
"I still want a job," he says to the boss.
"Did you get a certificate?" asks the boss.
"I did not get a certificate," Brad says.
"Look, man, you got to get a certificate.
It is just six months of school."
Brad still has some cash from his bad job with Trent.

Brad goes back to the welding school.
"I want to get into the class for the certificate," he says.
"OK," says the woman. "There is a class next week."
Brad gets into the class. He hands her the cash.
Then he calls his mom.
"Mama?" he says. "Do you still want to send the girls to the US?"
"Yes, Brad! They must get to the US."
"Mama, I just need six months.
You can send them to the US in six months."
At last, Brad is proud.

Ying

Chapter One

This is Ying.
Ying is from China.
When Ying was a kid, she lived in a small town
    in China.
From when she was very small, she did not want
    to be on a farm or in a small town.
She said, "Is this all there is?
Pigs and crops and plants?
I want lots of fun things in life, and pretty things."

When Ying was 17, she went to Hong Kong.
Hong Kong is a part of China. There are a lot of jobs and cash.
There are men and women from all over the world.
Ying was glad to be in a big, fast city.
She got a good job in a bank.
She felt a big rush to be in Hong Kong, with such a good job.
And she was in love with all the pretty things in the shops.
But Ying did still want more!

Ying met a man. His name was Sun Wen.
"You can call me Wen," he said.
Wen was from the US.
He had a big shop in New York City.
He was in Hong Kong with a long list of things he had to get
    for the shop.

"Oh!" said Ying. "Pretty things? Gifts and such?"
"No," said Wen. "Not pretty things. Things for the house.
Mops and pans, stuff like that."

Ying was so glad she had met a man who ran a shop.
This was a thing she would want to do.
"How did you get the shop?" she asked Wen.
"How do you run it?
What is it like to be in New York City?"
She had a lot of things to ask Wen.
She had a plan to have a shop of her own.

Ying was glad to help Wen find the things for his shop.
They went all over Hong Kong.
They went to shops and factories.
They put bids on lots of goods.
Wen was glad to get this help from Ying.
Ying was good at all the parts of this job.

At last, Wen had all the things for his shop.
He still had a day left in Hong Kong.
He went to find Ying.
He liked Ying. He liked Ying A LOT.
She had such a good mind.
She was full of zest and fun.
"I think she would like New York City,"
    Wen said.
"And she would be good in the shop."

Wen took Ying to the falls.

They took a bus, and then they went on foot the rest of the way
    to this beautiful spot.

Ying said, "I wish you did not have to go back to the US."

Wen said, "I must get back to the shop.

But . . . there is one thing left that I still must find."

Ying said, "What is that? I will help you find it!"

Wen held out a box with a ring in it.

He said, "Well . . . I still must find a wife."

Ying had to gasp as she held the ring.

Did she want to be Wen's wife?

And go to the US? And live in New York City?

And run a shop with Wen?

Of course she did!

This was what she had wanted ever since she was small.

"Yes!" she said with a yell. "I will be your wife!"

Chapter Two

Now Ying is Wen's wife!

She has a job in Wen's shop in the US.

She has to help Wen stock the shelf.

She has to help Wen run the shop.

It is a big shop.

The shop sells things for the house, things from China.

In China, Ying was bold.

She did all kinds of things in life.

She was not afraid.
Ying was bold and glad and full of zest and fun.
In New York City, Ying is not Ying.
She is afraid.

"You must ask the people in the shop if they want help," says Wen.
"You act all shy," he says.
(When Wen and Ying chat with each other, it is in Chinese.)
"You must ask them how they are. And if they want help.
You must say, 'Hello! How are you? Can I help you
    find something?'"
But Ying will not ask the people if they want help.
She will not even say hello.
In the US, Ying is shy and afraid.

Now Wen is mad at Ying.
"What is up with you? You must talk to the people!"
"I can't do it!" says Ying with a big sob.
"I can not talk to them. I can not talk in English!"
Wen stops. "What? Yes, you can. In Hong Kong you could talk
    in English."

Ying says, "In Hong Kong, I had a small bit of English,
     just enough for the job.
It was OK in Hong Kong. This is the US.
Here, I do not have enough English."

Wen is the kind of man who wants to fix a problem.
"Oh! It is the English!" he says.
"Well, that is not a bad thing. You can just get a book.
You can fix this problem. I will get you a book to learn English."
Wen is the kind of man who will do things by himself.
He gets Ying a book. He is glad this problem is all set.

Ying is glad she has a book.
At last she can get good at English.
She sits with the book and does her best.
She sits with the book all day in the shop.
And all night she sits with the book in her lap.

After six months, she still can not talk in English.
She still can not talk to the men and women in the shop.
Wen is mad at her a lot.
Ying is mad at Wen.
She should not have left Hong Kong!

"I can not talk in English!" she yells at Wen.
"And this shop is bad! There are no beautiful things in the shop!
I have nothing to do in the US.
All I do is sell mops and pans.
I want to go back to Hong Kong!"

Chapter Three

Ying is all set to go back to Hong Kong.
No more US! No more shop! No more Wen!
But then the best thing happens.
A Chinese-American woman is in the shop.
"Hello," she says in English. "Can you help me?"
Ying just shrugs. She still can not talk in English.
"Oh!" says the woman. "Do you need help with English?"

The Chinese-American woman gets out a pen
    and a pad.
"My mom did not talk in English for 15 years!"
    she says.
"Then she went to this class. It is a good class!
You should go to this class."
She hands Ying the pad.
"Go here," she says in Chinese. "Learn English!"
Ying nods. "OK," she says. "I will go."

Ying goes to the class.
She is so glad to be in a class!
A book is not the best way to get good English. A class will help!
In the hall, Ying finds a woman who is lost. It is Clem.
"Come!" she says to Clem. "Let's go to English class!"
They go to the class together.

But when she is in the class, Ying still will not talk.
The teacher calls on her. "Hello, Ying! How are you today?"

Ying gets red and will not talk.
At home she tells Wen. "I still can not talk in class."
"Why not?" asks Wen.
"I am still not good in English," Ying says.
"I want to talk in English only when I am the best."

"Ying," says Wen, "You can not get good in English
　　if you do not talk."
Wen tells her how, when he was a kid, and got to the US,
　　he did not talk in English.
"But then I had to talk in English.
The gas man was at the door, and my mother and father
　　could not talk in English.
So I had to talk.
And then the teacher, and the landlord, and the cop,
　　and lots and lots of people.
I had to do all the talking."
Soon, Wen was good at English.
"It is OK to mess up," Wen told Ying.
"When you mess up, you learn. It is OK.
You must mess up in English, and then you will learn!"

Ying gets this.
I have to mess up, she thinks.
But it is hard.
Ying thinks, *I need a pal to chat with.*
She calls Clem to ask.
"My English still so bad," she says.
"You help me? Chat with me?"

Clem is glad to help.
Clem and Ying get coffee and chat in English.
Ying can mess up in front of Clem.
She knows Clem does not mind.
Then, a man from the class asks if he can chat with them.
Then, a woman from the class asks.
Soon, Ying and Clem have a group that gets coffee
    and chats in English.
Ying loves this. She chats in English—and she has pals!

At last, Ying will talk in English, in the shop and in class.
And on the bus and at the park and in the book shop. Everywhere!
"Hello! Ying says to the people in the shop. "How are you?
    Can I help?"
At the park she says, "Hello! Happy good day!"
At the book shop she says, "Good day. I look book for husband.
    You help me?"
On the bus she says, "Hello. Thank you. Help me find stop
    for Elm Street. Please."
Ying is glad to be in New York City, with a job in the shop,
    and with her pals, and with her good man Wen.

Chapter Four

Ying still goes to English class. But now her English is very good.
She chats in English to all the people she finds.
This helps her to get better and better.
Now that she can talk in English, she is the old Ying again.
This is the Ying that wants fun.

The Ying that wants new things all the time.
Ying is back!

Ying is glad to work in the shop, and chat with the people.
She helps Wen pick out new things to sell in the shop.
She goes with Wen back to Hong Kong on trips to get stuff
    for the shop.
She tells Wen, "We should sell snacks in the shop!
The kind of snacks that you get in Hong Kong."
Wen thinks this is a good plan.
He puts in a snack bar, and they sell Hong Kong snacks and drinks.

But Ying still wants more.
"Wen," she says, "I want something more, but I am not sure what."
What can Wen do? He can not stop her!
Ying tells Wen, "I got into a class.
It is for people who want to run a business."
"But we already run a business."
Ying shrugs. "But I want more. I want a bigger business."
Wen says, "OK, good luck." He can not stop Ying!

In her class, Ying has to make a plan for a new business.
Her plan is for a gift shop.
It is the shop she has had in her mind since she was a small child.
Ying loves the plan for this beautiful shop.
She puts everything she has into the plan for this shop.
She works out all parts of the shop, even how much
    everything would cost, down to the last penny.

When the plan is done, Ying goes to Wen.
"Wen," she says, "I have a plan for a shop.
The shop would sell all the stuff I miss from Hong Kong.
Pretty things, and stuff for dress-up, and beautiful gifts.
A shop for women, with tea and cakes. A pretty shop.
And look," she says. "I have all the cash worked out,
    down to the last penny."
Wen says, "Hmmm. Not bad."

Wen and Ying do not have the cash to rent a spot for Ying's shop.
"So," says Ying, "what if we put my shop in the back of this shop?"
This is not what Wen had in mind for his shop.
But Ying knows it is the best way.
She shows Wen her plan again.
All the cash works out, down to the last penny.
At last, Wen grins and says, "Let's give it a shot."

Ying has set up a small shop in the back end of the big shop.
It is beautiful. She sells pretty gifts and beautiful things.
She brings in cakes from another shop, and sells them there.
People love Ying's shop!
"Soon we can rent a new spot just for your shop," says Wen.
He is proud of his wife. And Ying is glad to be in the US with Wen.

Greg

Chapter One

This is Greg.
Greg has no job.
Two years back, his wife, Shell,
    won a visa to the US.
Back then, Greg had a job, and so he did not go.
But now there are no jobs.

Greg's mom and dad went to school.
But Greg did not.
When Greg was a kid, there was a war.
The schools did not last in the war.
They all shut down.
So Greg did not go to school.

Still, Greg can do a lot of things.
He can read and do math.
He has a truck, and he can drive it.
He can dig a well.
He can fix a car.
He can run a shop.
He knows English, French, and the language of his people.
But there are no jobs for any of these things.

Greg's plan is to go the US.
To do this, he must get a visa.
This is how to get a visa:
He goes to the Embassy.
A lot of men and women are there.
He gets in line with them.

The line lasts all day.
At the end of the day, a woman asks Greg to come with her.
"At last, it is you," she says.
She brings him to a man at a desk.
This man has all the visas.
It is all up to him.

"Why do you want to go to the US?"
    he asks Greg.
Greg says, "My wife won a visa.
She is there with my kids.
My wife says she can get me a job."
The man asks, "Why did you not go when she went?"
Greg says, "I had a job then. I had to finish the job."

The man picks up his stuff.
He checks his watch.
At last he says, "No visa for you."
He shrugs, and then gets up to go.
Greg puts his face in his hands.

Greg walks back home.
He passes shops that are shut down.
He passes kids that ask him for cash so they can eat.
He passes men who just sit and watch him pass.
He passes all this.
He thinks, *This can not last.*

Chapter Two

Greg is on the phone with his wife, Shell.
"I did not get the visa," he says.
Shell says, "Did you tell them I am here?"
"Yes, I told them."
"Did you tell them the kids are here?"
"Yes, I told them."
"Did you tell them I can get you a job?"
"Yes, I told them."

Shell is upset. She sobs to Greg.
"Greg, I can not do this with you still
    back home.
The kids must have a dad,
    and I must have a husband.
I can not get the cash for the rent,
    and still be with the kids.
I can not get to the job when I must
    pick up the kids at school.
I have no mom or gran to help me.
I can not do this without help from you."

Greg thinks to himself, *This can not last*.
He says to Shell, "I will get to the US.
I will get to the US with or without a visa.
I must get there.
I can not trust that I will ever get a visa."
Shell says, "Be careful!"

Greg goes to a bar.
He finds a man at the bar.
The man has a black hat, and a ring in his left ear.
"Can you help me?" he asks the man.
The man shrugs. "Tell me what you want."
"I want to get to the US, but I can not get a visa."

The man brings Greg to the back of the bar.
"Shh," he says. "This is what I can do.
I can get you a visa and an ID.
I can sell you a spot on a ship that will get you to New York.
But it is a bad trip. There is a lot of risk."
"How much will it cost?" asks Greg.
"Two grand," says the man.

What can Greg say?
He must to get to New York, to be with his wife and kids.
He must get a job.
Here, he can not find a job, and he can not be with his wife
    and kids.
But it is a bad trip with a lot of risk.
"OK," he tells the man. "I will do it."

Greg sells his truck.
He sells all the stuff he has.
He gets all the cash he has in the bank.
He asks his pals to lend him cash.
"I will send it back to you from the US," he says.
He gets the two grand.

At dusk, he finds the man in the black hat.
He hands the man the cash.
"OK," says the man. "Just a few things I must tell you.
Get to the dock at 4 AM on Sunday. Find the man with the red cap.
Tell him that I sent you.
He will put you into the hold of the ship.
When you get into the hold, you must not say a thing.
If you say just one thing, they will kill you.
Do you get this?
They will not get stuff for you to eat.
You must bring nuts and water. That is all. Good luck."
And he is gone.

Chapter Three

It is 4 AM on Sunday.
Greg is all set for his big trip. He is at the dock.
But where is the man with the red cap?
Oh. There he is.
"Hey man," Greg calls to him.
The man stands up and calls back to him.
"Hush, man! Shut up!"

"You can call me Josh," says the man in the red cap.
"But do not call me! Do not say a thing to me."
Greg nods.
"You have water and nuts?"
Greg nods.
"The trip is 20 days. We will stop at a dock here and there.
You must not say a thing.
If they check the hold, you must not say a thing.
If they find you, they will kill you.
Got it?"
Greg nods.

Day 1
It is all black in the hold.
The ship hums and rocks.
Greg is next to casks of goods.
There is no one in the hold with him.
Just lots of rats.
This will be a bad trip.

Day 4
The ship stops. The hum of the ship stops.
The waves lap at the ship.
They must be at a dock.
Men chat in the hall by the hold
    where Greg is.
Greg holds his breath.
The trap door swings open.
A flash of light swings by Greg.
But Greg does not say a thing,
    and then the door shuts.

Day 10
Greg wants a fresh drink so bad.
His water is old and hot.
And he can just have a sip of it so that it will last.
He is sick of nuts.
He is sick of this trip.
All he can do is think of how it will be when he gets to the US.
He thinks of his wife and his kids.

Day 15
Crash! Bang! Smash!
It must be a storm.
Greg holds on to the cask.
He can not do a thing.
The ships rocks back and forth.
It jumps up and then sinks down and then jumps back up.
Ohhh. Oh God. Help me, God. I have no strength.
Greg is so sick of this.

Day 20
The hum of the ship stops.
Then the ship stops.
The trap door swings open.
"Hey man." It is Josh, the man in the red cap.
"Are you still with us?"
Greg wants to sob. 20 days is too much.
"We had good luck, man," says Josh.
"Just one storm, and it was not too bad.
And the cops did not mess with us."

Josh brings Greg out of the ship onto the dock.
Greg is so glad to be out of the ship!
But he is thin and weak. His legs are not strong. He has no fat left.
"Okay, man," says Josh. "That is it."
"What do I do now?" asks Greg. "Where do I go?"
Josh shrugs. "I don't know. Find your wife."
Greg nods. "Yes," he says. "Yes, I will find my wife."
At last, after 20 days in the hold of the ship, he can see the sky.
He can see the moon. He holds his hands up to the sky.
His chest is full. He grins.
"I must find my wife."

Chapter Four

Greg is stuck.
He got to the US! This is a big thing!
He is in the Bronx.
And now he must find Shell, his wife.
When he left, Shell said, "Call me when you get to the US.
    I will pick you up."
The plan was that Greg would call her on a pay phone.
But Greg can not find a pay phone.

OK, first things first: a snack.
He has a bit of cash.
"Good morning!" he says to the man at the food truck.
"Good morning to you," says the man. "What can I get you?"
Greg has had just nuts for 20 days.
The food truck has all kinds of things, like eggs on a roll, hot dogs,
    and fish and chips.

Greg can not pick which thing to get. He wants them all!
At last he picks: an egg on a roll and a drink.
Ahhh. "This is the best!" he tells the man.

Now that he has had a snack, Greg must find his wife.
He has some coins.
But he can not find a pay phone.
He asks the man at the food truck.
"Where is there a pay phone?"
The man acts like Greg is nuts.
"A pay phone?" he yells. He cracks up.
"A pay phone. This kid wants a pay phone.
No pay phones, man! You have to get a cell phone!"
"I have a cell phone," says Greg, "but not an American cell phone."

The man at the food truck tells Greg to check at the shop.
Greg asks at the kid in the shop, "Do you have a pay phone?"
They have no pay phone.
"What do I do? Where can I find a phone? I must call my wife."
"You can call her on my phone."
The kid in the shop holds out his hand, with his phone, to Greg.
"Thank you, kid. Thank you, thank you!"

Greg calls Shell.
The phone rings and rings.
At last, Shell says, "Hello, this is Shell. I can not get to the phone.
Tell me who you are, and I will call you back."
"Shell, it is Greg. I am here! I will call you again."
He hangs up.

Greg thinks the best thing is to set out and find Shell's house.
He gets out his billfold and the scrap of paper with Shell's address.
"How do I get here?" he asks the kid in the shop.
"Oh man, that is a long trip," says the kid.
"I think you want to get the bus."
"Where do I get the bus?"
"There is a stop at the end of this street."
"Do I pay with cash?"
"No," says the kid. "You must have a card. You can have this one.
Just give me five bucks for it."
"Thanks, kid!"

Greg gets on the bus.
At last he can rest.
He just has to watch for his stop.
He slumps down in his seat.
His head rests on the glass.
His eyes shut.
Greg is asleep.
When Greg wakes up, it is dusk
    outside.
What the heck?!
Where is he?
He jumps up and runs to the front of the bus.
"Excuse me!" he says. "Did I miss my stop?"
He holds out the scrap of paper with Shell's address.
The man checks the scrap of paper.
"It's OK, man. Your stop is next."

Greg gets off at the next stop.

He checks the scrap of paper.

56 Elm Street.

Just two blocks.

He runs most of the way.

It is the last stretch of his long, long trip.

He gets to 56 Elm Street and rings the bell.

"Yes?" The door opens just a crack.

"Shell? It is me!"

"Greg?"

The door swings all the way open.

From one end of the block to the other end, all the people
on Elm Street can hear the glad shouting and clapping
of Greg and Shell and their kids.

Grant

Chapter One

This is Grant.
Grant is from Somalia.
When he was 20, Grant left Somalia.
His mom and dad had left Somalia too.
Grant left Somalia, and went to the US
    to be with his mom and dad.

When Grant got to the US, his plan was to go to school.
But that plan fell through.
He had to get a job.
He got a job in a hospital. He has had this job for three years.
Grant is sad that he did not go back to school.
But when his job is done, he wants to rest, not study!
He wants to watch TV and rest.

Grant has a wife, Fran.
Fran is from Somalia, too.
Fran does not want to rest, ever!
She is on the go, all day long.
She is bold and strong.
She went back to school.
Now she gets more cash than Grant.
Grant is OK with this.
But Fran is not OK with it. She has big plans for Grant!

First, Fran thinks Grant must go back to school.
"Grant," she says, "don't you want a job that gets you more cash?"
"Yes, I do," says Grant. "But it is such a long trip to get there.
I would have to do a lot of tests.
At the end of the day, I am spent.
I just want to rest."

This is not OK with Fran.
"Is that your *plan?*" she asks.
"I just want to chill and rest," says Grant with a shrug.
"When I am on the job, I work hard. Then I go home, and I rest."
When Fran is mad, she will stand up and cross her arms.
This is what she does now.
"You must do the test for the diploma," she says.
"Do you get it?"

At last Grant shrugs.
"Okay, he says. "I will do it."
He gets a book to prep for the test.
He finds a class.
For six months, he preps for the test.
Math, English, science.
He preps for all of it.
Fran helps him.
Grant is good in class—
    when he studies.
Fran is glad. "You will pass this test,"
    she says with a nod.
"I am sure of it."

At last, Grant goes for the test.

It is a long test—7 hours.

When he is done, the man tells him the good news.

"Good job," he says. "You got a pass. You will get a diploma."

Grant goes out of the test room and calls Fran.

"Fran!" he says. "I did it!"

"That is great! You are the best!" says Fran.

"And it was not so bad, to prep for that test, was it?" asks Fran.

"No," says Grant. "It was not so bad.

"Good," says Fran. "Because this is not the end.

Now you must go on."

"What?" says Grant. "Go on?"

For a month, Grant thinks about his plans.

Fran wants him to go on with school.

She wants him to go to college so he can be a nurse.

If he does this, he will have to be in class for a long time.

But he does not think he can say no to Fran.

And he thinks he would not mind school so much.

He goes home.

"Fran?" he calls. "Baby, I must tell you something. Something big!"

Fran says. "Hold on. I must tell you something.

Something even bigger."

Chapter Two

Grant passed his test. Now he has a high school diploma.

He wants to tell his wife his big plan—that he wants
    to go back to school to be a nurse.

But his wife, Fran, has to tell him something, too.

"What is it?" he asks Fran.
Fran holds up a different kind of test.
"You are going to be a dad."

Grant does not get it.
"A dad?" he says. "What?"
"Yes, a dad," says Fran.
"And I will be a mom."
"No, that can not be!" yells Grant.
"My plan is to go back to school!
I want to go back to school to be a nurse."
"OK, Daddy," says Fran.
"You can be in school.
In fact, you *must* be in school.
But you will be a daddy, too."

Grant thinks for a bit.
Then it hits him.
He jumps up and yells. "A dad! I am going to be a dad!"
He picks up Fran and spins her around
    and plants a big kiss on her lips.
"I am so glad! You will be the best mom!
We will have the best kid!"
He spins her around and around.
"Wow!"

This is the plan:
Grant will prep for the test to get into college.
He will still be at his job.
Fran will still be at her job, too.

Grant and Fran will work and work. And work and work.
They must get a lot of cash, for when the baby comes.
And Grant *must* pass that test.
"This baby can not have a dad who can not get a good job,"
    says Fran.

Fran and Grant have dinner with Grant's mom and dad.
"How is the baby?" they ask. They grin at Fran and hug her.
They are so glad about this baby.
Fran pats her belly. "Getting big," she says. She grins back at them.
Grant pats Fran's belly. "We will be glad when this baby gets here!"
Fran nods. "Things will be good when the baby gets here.
We will not be so tired."
"Yes," says Grant. "Then we can rest with the baby."
Grant's mom grins at Grant's dad. He just grins and shrugs.
"They will find out," says Grant's dad.
"Let them find out on their own."

Grant is on his way to class.
"Grant, hold on a sec," says Fran.
"I have to go to the doctor on Friday. Can you go with me?"
"Why?" asks Grant. "Is it all OK?"
He pats Fran's belly. Her belly got so big!
"Yes," says Fran. "It is all OK.
It is just that I must get a test to check on the baby.
And we will be able to see the baby!
And we can find out if it is a boy or a girl."
Grant grins and nods. "I can miss class for that!"

Grant and Fran are at the hospital. Fran is on her back on the bed.
The woman from the hospital checks her belly.
She has a stick that she puts on Fran's belly.
Then they all watch the screen to see the baby.
"Look!" says the woman. "You can see the head, and the legs,
    and the . . . Oh. Oh my god."
"What is it? What is it?" yells Grant. "Is it something bad?"
"I must get the doctor!" The woman runs from the bed.

The woman comes back with the doctor.
The doctor checks the screen.
"Oh, wow," she says. She nods at the woman.
"What? What is it?" says Fran. Grant can not say a thing.
The woman and the doctor grin.
"Everything is OK," says the doctor. "But you have twins in here."
Twins?!
Twins!

Chapter Three

Grant and Fran are having twins.
What a shock!
But the shock will pass.
And now Grant has big plans for the twins.
They will go to school.
They will be the best kids in the class.
They will do well on tests.
Grant thinks a lot about his kids.
He should prep for his big test, but he just wants to think
    about the twins.

Grant tells Fran, "Nothing will stop these kids.
They will go all the way to the top."
On some days he thinks, "Doctors.
They will be doctors. They will help the world."
On some days he thinks, "No, they will have top jobs in the banks.
They will have lots of cash."
Then, on some days he thinks, "Teachers.
They will be teachers in school, and bring up the kids."
Fran shrugs. "I just want strong babies with good health."
Then she grins at Grant.
"OK, a job in the bank would not be bad."

Grant must get back to his test prep.
His class is done, and now it is up to him to study by himself.
But all he wants to do is think about the twins.
Fran finds him on the bed. His eyes are shut.
"Grant!" Fran yells.
He sits up in bed. "What?! What?!"
"You must study for the test! What is up with you?
Stop it! Do not think about the twins. Think about the test!"

Fran frets that if Grant does not study, that they will be stuck
    with no cash for the rest of the their lives.
"If he can not pass that test, I will be so mad!"
    she says to her pal, Pam.
"You must let him know that this is a big thing for you," says Pam.
"Oh, he knows. He knows."

Grant knows that Fran will be mad if he can't pass the test.
This gets him upset.

What if he can't pass it?
Will she kick him out?
Grant is so upset he can not study for the test.

Fran's belly is so big.
It is hot out, and she can not sleep.
She will toss and fret all night.
And Grant can not study.
They are up all night.
"I can't sleep," says Fran. "It is too hot!"
"I can't study," says Grant.

"Let's go up to the top of the house," says Fran, "to the roof.
It is not so hot up there."
They bring a thick, soft pad up to the roof.
They stretch out on it.
"Fran," says Grant. "What if I can not pass the test? Will you be mad?
I am not sure I can pass it."

Fran puts Grant's hand on her belly.
One of the twins kicks at his hand.
"Ouch!" yells Grant with a big grin. "That is a strong baby!"
"Yes," says Fran. "They are strong babies.
And they need a strong mom and dad.
Grant, if you can not pass the test, it is OK.
But I will be mad if you do not study.
You must study. You must try!"
Grant nods. The baby kicks at his hand. That kick fills him with joy.
He hugs Fran. "I will do anything for these babies," he says.
"I will study."

Chapter Four

Everyone is so glad that there will be twins!
At the job, there is a big party.
For the gifts, there are two of every gift.
"Twins!" everyone says.
"Watch out!" They wink and grin.
Grant and Fran just sit
    and say thanks to all.
They are so tired.

"Boys or girls?" everyone asks.
Grant and Fran just shrug.
"We did not find out," they say.
"When they told us we had twins,
    we did not find out the sex."
Grant and Fran go to a child birth class.
They watch a film.
The film tells how the birth will go.
Fran can watch a film like this. She is strong!
Grant can not watch a film like this.
He feels sick.

At the end of Grant's class, he will have the test.
The test will be on August 1.
The babies will come on August 15.
Grant studies on the job. He studies on the bus.
He studies in the bath. He studies all the time!
He will not stop.
He will do anything for those babies.

The test is today!

Grant drinks his coffee. But where is Fran?

Fran is still in bed.

"The babies," she says with a grin. "I think they want to come."

"What?! Now? No! They still have two weeks in there!"
   yells Grant.

"I can not tell them that," Fran says.

"They will come when they want to come. Babies are like that."

"But my test!"

Fran thinks for a bit.

"Let's get a cab," she says. "You will drop me off at the hospital.
And then go on to the test.

Come back to the hospital when the test is done."

Fran is strong and bold. And she knows Grant must pass that test!

Grant drops Fran off at the hospital.

He wants to come in and help her to the wing
   where babies are born.

But then he will be late to the test.

"Just GO!" says Fran. She gives him a kiss and a hug. "Good luck."

Grant goes to the test.

It is a long test. He can not think of Fran, or of the babies!

At the end of the test, he gets to find out how he did.

And then he runs back to the hospital!

In the hospital he runs to the wing where babies are born.

There is no one at the desk.

He checks in all the rooms. "Fran? Fran? Where are you?"

"Hey, bud," says a man with a mop. "You want some help?"

"Yes, I can not find my wife! She is here to have twins!"

"Oh!" says the man with the mop. "You are the dad of the twins!
Everyone is in that room with the twins and the mom.
That room there. Room 6."
"Thank you!"

Grant runs to Room 6.
He finds Fran in bed, with two babies.
Two beautiful, small babies.
"Look, Grant! Two girls! Here is Daddy, girls."
Grant can not say a thing.
Fran hands him a baby.
He sits and holds her.
"Wow. Just . . . wow."

"And the test, Papa?"
"What do you think, Mama?"
"I think you passed."
Grant puts one hand on the back of the baby's head.
Her black hair is soft, and her beautiful black eyes look up at him.
He puts his hands on her ears.
Then, at last, he puts his head back and lets out a soft yell.
"YES! I passed! I passed that test!"
His heart fills with all the joy that one man's heart can hold.

Jinx

Chapter One

This is Jinx.
Jinx is from the Bronx, in New York City.
Jinx has a job in a bank.
She is good at her job.

Jinx's boss, Kent, is glad that Jinx is there.
Jinx hands in her work on time.
Jinx is good and kind with the men and women
    who come to the bank.
Jinx is a star at the job.

When Jinx is not at the job, she has fun.
She has two men she tends to go out with.
Frank is a good man. He is kind and sweet.
Mark is a good man, too.
He is handsome and has a lot of flash and bling.

When Jinx is out with Frank, they have a lot of fun.
It is a sweet kind of fun.
They go on picnics. They go to the park.
They go to hang out with their pals.

Frank has a big family.
The people in his family are kind and sweet.
They are just like Frank.
The kids are glad when Jinx is with Frank.
They say, "Jinx is here!"

It is not like this when Jinx is out with Mark.
Mark and Jinx go into the city.
They go to clubs.
They will watch a film and then get a drink at some hot spot
    in the city.

Jinx will dress up when she goes out with Mark.
She puts on a dress.
She and Mark will go to a jazz club.
It is so much fun to be with Mark.

Jinx says to her pal Beth, "How can I pick just one man?
They are both good men."
Beth shrugs.
"Just hold on to both."
But Jinx thinks this is not
    a good plan.
I must pick just one man,
    she thinks.

Chapter Two

One day, Frank calls.
He says, "Let's go to the park."
"What is at the park?" Jinx asks.
Frank says, "My mom and dad and all the kids.
It is a big picnic. It will be a lot of fun!
They all want to see you!"

Jinx and Frank go to the park.
Frank's mom hugs Jinx and says, "I am so glad to see you!"
Frank's dad says, "Jinx! Help me with this kite!"
Frank's sis, Jill, asks Frank for help with her baby.
"Fuss, fuss, fuss!" says Jill.
"Frank, this baby just wants to fuss all day long."
Jill knows that Frank is the best with kids.
Frank holds the baby and sings and chats with him.

Jinx sits with Frank.
"You are so good with kids," she says.
"Oh, thanks," says Frank.
"It is not hard to be good with kids," he shrugs.
"Do you think you want to have kids?" Jinx asks.
"That is the plan," says Frank, with a big grin.

The next night, Jinx goes out with Mark.
They get drinks at a jazz club in the city.
Jinx is in a dress that has a lot of flash.
At the club, Jinx asks Mark what he wants to do
    with the rest of his life.

"I want to be in films," he says. "I want to act.
I want to be a big star in big films."
Mark is handsome with a lot of flash.
Jinx thinks Mark can do this.

"Well," says Jinx, "what about kids?"
"Kids?" Mark says, as if he does not know what kids are.
"Yes, kids," says Jinx. "A baby? Kids?"
"Oh, kids. No," says Mark, with his hand up. "No kids."
"I have big plans to be a star. I can not have kids."
"Oh," says Jinx.
She did not know this about Mark, that he did not want kids.

Mark looks at Jinx and holds her hand.
"I want you to be with me," he says.
Mark has a lot of flash and wants to be a big star,
    but he is still kind.
If Jinx is with Mark, she will have a glam life with a kind man.
Just no kids.
But Jinx can not say a thing.
She gasps. Frank is here!

"Frank! What are you doing here?"
Frank says, "What are YOU doing here?"
Jinx says, "I am with Mark. Mark, this is Frank.
    Frank, this is Mark."
Jinx says, "But, Frank, this is not your kind of spot."
Frank says, "I am with my pals. My pal Rick is into
    this kind of thing."
He shrugs. "So here we are."

Frank says, "What are you doing here with this man?
Jinx says, "Frank, you are not the only man I see."
But Frank is upset.
He says, "This can not go on. You must pick one of us."
Mark shrugs and says, "I am chill, baby.
You do not have to pick just one of us."
But Jinx thinks Frank is right. She must pick one man.

Chapter Three

Jinx is sick of this mess.
She thinks Frank is right. She must pick a man.
But which man is the best?
Frank is so kind and good.
But Mark is so handsome and has a lot of flash!
Frank wants kids. Mark wants no kids.
What is the best thing to do?

The thing with Jinx is, she has no mom or dad.
Her mom died when she still small. And she did not know her dad.
Jinx was with her Gran.
Her Gran was good and kind and had lots of love for Jinx.
Jinx had hugs and love all day long from her Gran.
But she did not have a big family.

When Jinx was a kid, her wish was to have a big family.
In the park she would see big picnics.
She would see kids and moms and dads.
Kids with a big family seemed like rich kids to Jinx.

This is what Jinx wants: a big family with lots of love.
It is the thing she wants most of all.

Jinx had another wish as well: she wants a good job.
Jinx has this.
She is a star at her job.
Her boss, Kent, says she will go far at the bank.
Jinx could mess this up if she has lots of kids.
Jinx thinks . . . *maybe one or two kids at most.*

Jinx asks her Gran which man to pick.
And which life to pick.
Gran will not tell her.
Gran just says, "Think of what you want most from this life.
Is it the glam life? Is it films and drinks and flash?
Or is it family? Kids and a good man and a good job?

Jinx thinks of life with Mark.
She will have lots of beautiful things.
She will go to films a lot.
She will get drinks with Mark.
She will have a lot of flash in her life.
She will be a star at her job,
    as she will not have kids to watch.

Then Jinx thinks of life with Frank.
She will go on picnics and go to the park.
She and Frank can have kids.
Not a lot of kids. Just one or two kids.

Then she can still be a star at her job.
She will not have a big family.
Oh. But wait! She will have Frank's big family.

Jinx calls Mark. "We must talk," she says.
She and Mark go to a spot on Elm Street for a drink.
Jinx and Mark have a long chat.
She tells Mark her wish for a big family.
She tells Mark her wish that he can act and be in films.
She and Mark hug and say good-bye.
Then, at last, Jinx calls Frank.

Chapter Four

This is it. Jinx wants to be with Frank.
Frank wants to be with Jinx.
And now . . . Jinx wants a ring.
Jinx is the kind of person who gets what she wants.
Jinx wants a ring.
So Jinx gets a ring.
Jinx gets a ring for Frank.
She will ask Frank to marry her.
Why not?
Should she sit and wait for Frank to get the ring and ask her?
No. Jinx does not want to wait!

Jinx wants to ask Frank to marry her.
So she must plan a surprise.
This is how you ask:

You plan a big thing, and then you pull out the ring,
    and then you ask for the hand.
This is Jinx's plan: She will ask Frank to go for dinner.
She will put the ring in his drink.
She thinks, *but what if he drinks the ring?*
OK. She will put the ring next to the glass.

There is this thing, dinner on a ship.
You get dinner and drinks on the ship.
The ship goes all around the city.
She calls Frank. "Let's go on this thing.
This dinner on a ship.
It is all set," she says. "Let's go, OK?"
But Frank says no. "Hon, I can't go on a ship."
"What? Why not?"
"Hon, I get sick on a ship. I can not get dinner on a ship."

Frank calls Jinx and says, "Let's go to the museum.
There is a thing I want to see."
But Jinx is still mad about her plan with the ship.
She says, "A museum?
Frank, I do not want to go to a museum."
Frank says, "Come on, Jinx. Let's go to the museum."
Jinx does not know this, but Frank has a ring, too.
Frank wants to give the ring to Jinx, and ask for her hand.
He has a plan, as well.

"Frank, let's have dinner in the city," says Jinx.
She thinks, *I can still put the ring next to the glass.*

But now Frank is upset.
"If you will not go to the museum," he says,
    "then I do not want to go to dinner in the city."
Now Jinx is upset.
"Well, if you will not go to dinner," she says,
    "then I do not want to go to the museum."
Frank and Jinx both hang up!

Frank calls Jinx.
He has a new plan.
"Hey baby," he says, "let's go to a baseball game."
Jinx is still mad, but the fact is, she loves baseball.
Jinx says, "Well, OK."
Frank's plan is that he will ask Jinx to marry him at the game.
It will be on the big TV screen at the game. It will be fun!

Frank gets to Jinx's house, to pick her up for the game.
"Who is at the game?" she asks.
"The Mets," says Frank.
"WHAT? The Mets?"
Jinx stops cold in her tracks.
"We can not watch the Mets.
    We are Yankees fans,
    Frank!"
Jinx will not watch the Mets.
And just like that,
    Frank's plan is over.

"Let's just go the park," says Frank.

At the park, Frank and Jinx get hot dogs and sit to watch
    a kids' baseball game.

"One day, that will be us, with our kids," says Frank.

"What?" says Jinx.

"Yes, Jinx, we will be together, yes?"

Frank holds out a box with a ring in it. "Will you marry me?"

Jinx has to rush to get out Frank's ring. "And will you marry me?"

As they hug and kiss, Frank says, "This is great, Jinx.

And now at last you can quit your job!"

"What??!"

Will Frank get it that Jinx wants to go far at the bank?
Is this marriage a bad plan?
Read to the end of Level 4 to find out!

Level 3
Aspen Street

The Men and Women of Aspen Street

Isad — a woman who wants to finish school
Jamal — a kid who is acting out in class
Kendrick — a kid with a lot of talent at basketball
Patrick — a man who goes back to the Dominican Republic
Isabel — a woman whose mom wants her to find a husband
Bethann — a woman who misses gardening with her granddad

Isad

Chapter One

This is Isad.
Isad has a job in a print shop.
She works hard. She has to.
Isad has two children, and no husband.
When her job is finished for the day,
    she goes to a second job.

Isad is an immigrant from Pakistan.
She got to the US when she was 17 years old.
She had just finished high school in Pakistan.
Her English was excellent.
Within in a few months, she got a job . . . and then a husband.

Isad and her husband Hassan worked hard.
They both had two jobs.
They worked all the time.
They were committed to their big plan: college for both of them.
"When you have a college diploma," Hassan said,
    "no one can ever take that from you."

Isad said, "You go first.
Then, when you have a good job, I will go."
So Hassan prepped for the college exam.

He passed the exam, and in September he began his classes.
Isad worked her two jobs to pay the bills.

It was all happening as they had planned.
Hassan was about to finish college.
Isad began to prep for the exam.
At last, she was going to college!
But then—something big, and unexpected, happened.
A baby.

Now Isad was home with the baby Lintah.
No college for Isad.
"So, we go with Plan B," said Hassan.
"When the child is in school, you will go to college.
You must accomplish this, Isad," he said.
"When you have a college diploma,
    it belongs to you forever."

But then there was another baby, Ifrah.
Two beautiful girls!

Isad and Hassan were glad they had to switch to Plan B.
"We are blessed," said Isad. She was in love with these babies.
"When Lintah and Ifrah are in school, you will go to college,"
    said Isad's husband.
"We are committed to this plan, yes?"

But luck was not always with Isad.
Lintah was six. Ifrah was four.
Hassan was struck by a bus, and killed in an instant.
All of a sudden, Isad and the girls were by themselves.
No father. No husband. No college degree.
There was nothing she could do, but work.

Chapter Two

Isad is strong and bold and committed to her girls.
All the years when they were getting big, she said to them:
"You must go to college.
When you have a college diploma,
    no one can ever take that from you.
We are committed to this plan, girls, yes?"

The girls were good in their classes.
Their mother worked so much.
They worked that much, too.
"Yes, Mama," they said.
"We are committed to this plan!"

Lintah was a strong student.
She ran track and was a star in the chess club.
She got into a college called Tufts.
"I am going to be a doctor," Lintah said.
She went off to college in Boston.
Isad was so, so proud.

Ifrah was also a strong student.
She did well in mathematics, but she also loved art.
"Mama," she said, "I want to go to college for art."
Isad did not think this was a good plan.
"Art?" she scoffed. "Ifrah, there are no jobs for artists."

Ifrah always did things in her own way.
"Mama, there are jobs for artists," she said.
"NO!" said Isad. "I did not work this hard for you to be an artist.
You must go to college for a subject that will get you a good job."
Ifrah sulked and fretted.

"You never let me do what I want!" Ifrah yelled at Isad.
"It is always what you want!
I am not Lintah. And I am not you!
I am sick of doing things just because you tell me to.
'Do math!' 'Do track!' 'Be the best!'"

Isad cannot understand what is happening.
All she has ever wanted was to go to college and have a good job.
When she could not do this, she wanted it for her daughters.

"This is the path to everything," she tells Ifrah.
"Why do you want to mess this up?"

At last Ifrah went to Isad with a plan.
"Mama," she said, "I will go to college for mathematics, OK?"
"But you must let me do art classes as well.
I will do both.
Just as you have always had two jobs, I will do two things
     at college.
Math and art."

Chapter Three

Isad and Ifrah had a plan.
Ifrah wanted to be an artist.
But she said she would go to school for math.
This would get her a good job.
And she would do art as well.

Isad said yes to this plan, and now Ifrah has gotten into
     Hunter College, in New York City.
All was happening as planned, after all.
Hassan would be so glad.
The girls were both in college.
Soon it would be Isad's turn.
Once again, she began to prep for the exam.
Once again, something unexpected happened . . .

Ifrah met a man. His name was Shakir.
Shakir was also from Pakistan. He planned to be a doctor.
Isad saw that Shakir would be a good husband.
She wanted to give Shakir and Ifrah her blessing for this marriage.
But she also wanted Ifrah to finish school.

Isad said to Ifrah, "You can get married.
But there is one thing. You must finish school!
Do not put your husband's school ahead of yours.
Your education is also important!"
Ifrah said, "I will finish school, Mama. I promise."

Soon, Ifrah was a married woman. Shakir was a good husband.
Ifrah was still in school, as she had promised.
And then, a year later, something happened . . .
"A BABY?" yelled Isad to Ifrah.
"You are having a BABY?"

"Mama, I can have a baby and still finish school," said Ifrah.
"You don't know how hard it is!" Isad yelled.
"You do not understand what happens with a baby.
All your plans get pushed back!"
She was so mad at Ifrah.
How could this child mess up everything
     that Isad and Hassan planned?

"What does Shakir say?" she asked.
Here, Ifrah began to cry.
"He says I should quit school."

Isad felt as if her world were falling to bits.
All these years of trying to get this one thing
    for herself and her girls have come to nothing.
She could not stop yelling, and Ifrah could not stop crying.

At last, Isad could yell no more.
She could almost hear her husband telling her,
    "Stick with the plan, Isad. Stick with the plan."
She had to get back to Plan B, just as she and Hassan had said.
Well, now it was Plan C. Or was it Plan D?
"You will NOT drop out of college," she told Ifrah.
"You tell Shakir to come talk to me."

Chapter Four

Three years have passed.
Lintah has finished college.
She is in medical school now.
She is on her way to becoming a doctor.
With that one, we did well, thinks Isad.

Ifrah is still in school.
She did not quit. And she is almost finished.
Ifrah's husband is almost finished with medical school.
Ifrah and Shakir have had so much help from Isad.
And still it is difficult.

As mad as she had been at Ifrah, Isad is in love with this little boy,
  her grandson, Hassan.
He is giggling and babbling all day.
He is beautiful.
He is the most fantastic baby.
But, wow, is she spent at the end of the day.

When she finishes her job, Isad rushes to pick up her grandson.
She brings him home, hugging and cuddling and chatting with him
  all the way.
She LOVES this little boy.
But she is so, so spent.
When Ifrah comes to pick up Hassan, she finds Isad
  crashed on the couch, with the boy chatting to himself.

When Ifrah or Shakir has an exam, Isad watches Hassan even more.
When he is sick, she is up with him.
When he is too sick for school, she skips work to be with him.
"I am too old for this," she says.
But she is on the path.
She is not getting off that path.

And now, at long last, the plan is almost finished.
Ifrah is finishing college!
She has finished her exams.
She did very well. But she left the math.
She has a job in the fall.
She will be an art teacher for small children.

At the graduation, Isad holds back tears.
"We did it, Hassan," she says, thinking of her husband.
She holds her hands up and lifts her face to the sky.
"Thank you, Allah!" she says.
"You can thank God all you want," says Ifrah.
"But I want to thank YOU, Mama."
She hugs her mother.

Ifrah's and Shakir's pals are giving a party, but Isad is not coming.
"Mama, you don't want to go to the party?"
"No," says Isad. "I have other plans."
Isad hands her beautiful grandson to her daughter.
"It's my turn," she says. "At long last, it is my turn."
And she goes back to the college campus to sign up for classes
    in the fall.

Jamal

Chapter One

Jonathan and Lindell
   have a kid.
Jamal is 9.
He is a terrific kid!
Clever! Smart!
But something is happening with Jamal.

In class, Jamal is having problems.
He can't sit still. He can't stop acting out.
He jumps up and yells out.
He can't stop himself.
The teacher is getting upset.

The teacher calls Lindell.
"We have to discuss Jamal," she says.
"He is becoming a big problem.
He is acting out too much in class.
This is a problem we have to discuss."

Lindell goes to the school to discuss Jamal.
She does not want to go.
Discussing her child with a teacher is not a good thing.

What is happening with Jamal?
Why is he acting out?

The teacher looks stressed.
"I have 30 kids in my class," she says.
"I can't help the kids with Jamal yelling and jumping around.
When we are attempting to get work finished, he is acting out.
It is a big problem."

"I will have a chat with Jamal," says Lindell.
"I will put a stop to this. I will punish him.
When I am done with Jamal, trust me, he will not act out in class."
When Lindell was a kid, kids did not act out.
Lindell intends to be very strict with Jamal.

The teacher looks distressed.
"I do not want you to punish him," she says.
"He is a good kid. He is not bad.
I think he cannot help himself."
"So what do you want me to do?" asks Lindell.

"I think he needs to go on pills," says the teacher.
"The pills will relax him in class. He will not act out."
"*Pills?*" Lindell is shocked.
"Yes, I think Jamal has ADD," says the teacher.
That's it. Lindell is finished with this teacher.
Her kid is not getting pills.
She rushes out of the class.

Chapter Two

Jonathan and Lindell are in conflict.
Jamal is acting out in class.
His teacher thinks he has ADD.
"ADD? What is ADD?" says Jonathan.
"It's when kids can't stop themselves from acting out,"
    says Lindell.
"I know what can stop a kid from acting out," says Jonathan.
He picks up his belt.

Lindell stops Jonathan.
"No," she says.
"Hitting him will not fix this problem."
"Well then, what should we do? Send him back home?
My grandmother can bring him up the old way.
Kids in the US do not understand how to act."
Lindell crosses her arms. "No.
We are not sending my boy back home."

"You would put Jamal on pills?" Jonathan says.
"This is how they fix problems in the US.
Just put the children on pills."
"No," says Lindell. "No pills."
"Well, then, what?"
Lindell thinks.
"We must have a chat with Jamal.
We must tell him this is a big problem.
When he understands,
    he will act better in class."

The chat does not go well.
Jonathan is yelling at Jamal.
"Son! This is a big problem!
We will send you back home if you do not act better!"
"I don't want to go back home," says Jamal.
He has never lived back home, just in the US.

Lindell attempts to get control of the chat.
"Jamal, we do not want to send you back home.
But you cannot act up in class.
You must sit still, and do what the teacher tells you.
Do you understand?"

Jamal says he will act better in class.
"I don't know why I can't sit still," he says.
He cannot understand it.
He was always one of the best kids in the class.
He could read and do math.
But all of a sudden, in third grade, school got difficult.

Jonathan and Lindell are glad that they had this chat.
They are content that the problem will be fixed.
"We just had to have this chat," says Lindell.
"Yes," says Jonathan. "He is a good son.
He will do well."

Lindell's cell phone rings.
"Hello?"
"Hello, Mrs. Kibet?"

"Yes?"
"This is Jamal's teacher.
You must come in.
The principal of the school wants to chat with you.
It is about Jamal."

Chapter Three

Lindell and Jonathan are in Jamal's class.
The teacher and the principal are with them.
"We are here to discuss Jamal," says the principal.
Her name is Mrs. Velasquez.
She looks competent and kind.

The teacher looks rushed and stressed.
"Jamal is a constant problem in the class," she says.
Mrs. Velasquez interrupts her.
"I did not want to begin this way," she says.
She looks back at Jonathan and Lindell.
"We want to find out what is best for Jamal."

"We know that Jamal is very smart.
We know that he did well in school until this year."
"Yes," says Lindell, nodding. "Something is different this year."
"So, what happened?" asks Mrs. Velasquez.
"Did something happen at home?"
Lindell and Jonathan think and then shrug.
"No, nothing is different at home."

"Jamal is in the third grade," says the principal.
"In third grade, lessons are different.
Kids don't *learn* to read. They *read* to learn.
If a child cannot read well, he or she may have problems
    in third grade.
Sometimes, these kids act out.
They would rather act like a problem kid, than be the kid
    who can't read."

"But Jamal loves to read," says Jonathan.
"When he was six years old, he could read all of his books."
Mrs. Velasquez says, "Sometimes, it looks like a child can read,
    but they are just remembering the words.
They cannot read new things.
They can only read the things they know."
Mrs. Velasquez looks at the teacher.
"Could it be that Jamal is struggling to read?"

The teacher looks stunned.

She did not think of this.

"It could be," she says at last.

She looks helpless. "I have 30 kids. It's hard to keep track."

She says, "I still think he should get put on pills."

"I do not think so," Mrs. Velasquez says.

To Jonathan and Lindell, she says, "This happens a lot.

These kids are good at distracting us from the real problem.

That is what the acting up is all about."

Jonathan is not OK with this.

"You're telling me my kid is stupid?"

"No," says Mrs. Velasquez. "We all know Jamal is
    a very smart child.

But if he is having a problem with reading,
    we must get him tested."

"We are not putting him on pills!" says Lindell in a strong voice.

"No, no pills," says Mrs. Velasquez.

"We will test him to find out if he has a problem with reading.

Then we will go from there."

Chapter Four

"Hello? Mrs. Kibet? This is Mrs. Velasquez.

I am calling to discuss the results of Jamal's test.

Can you come in on Monday after school?"

"Yes," says Lindell. "Monday is good."

More visits with the principal!

Again, Lindell and Jonathan and Mrs. Velasquez and the teacher
sit down to chat.
But now there is another person.
"Mr. and Mrs. Kibet," says Mrs. Velasquez, "this is
Mrs. Robinson.
She does the testing at the school."
They all say hello.

"So, the testing is finished.
And Mrs. Robinson will tell us her findings."
"Yes," says Mrs. Robinson, shuffling through the test results
in front of her.
"So, Jamal did well on most of the test. Yes, very well!
He is a very, very smart kid.
He is well past the third grade level on most of the test."
Lindell and Jonathan sit up and listen with new interest.
They did know they had been slumping.

"But there is a part of the test that did not go well.
Jamal has significant problems with reading."
Lindell and Jonathan slump back down and stop grinning.

Mrs. Robinson is not finished.
"There is so much contrast in Jamal's test
results.
On the one hand, he is past his grade level.
On the other hand, he is a struggling reader.
This is very interesting."

Mrs. Velasquez interrupts.

"Yes, and so we think that Jamal is dyslexic," she says.

"Dyslexic? What is dyslexic?" asks Lindell.

"It is a common problem," says Mrs. Robinson.

"When a child is on grade level, or past grade level,
    but just missing this one thing.

This thing called reading."

"But why can't he read," asks Lindell, "if he is so smart?"

"We don't know the exact cause of dyslexia," says Mrs. Robinson.

"We know the mind of a dyslexic child thinks in a different way.

Sometimes it can be wonderful.

Some very talented people are dyslexic.

But reading can be difficult."

"So what do we do?" asks Jonathan. "My son *must* learn to read."

"This is our plan," says Mrs. Velasquez.

"Jamal will stay in his class.

But every day, he will go to work with Mrs. Robinson.

They will work on reading.

Most kids get it together by the end of the year.

Jamal will be fine."

"What about pills?" asks the teacher.

"No pills!" say Mrs. Velasquez, Mrs. Robinson, Lindell,
    and Jonathan, all together.

Kendrick

Chapter One

This is Kendrick.
Kendrick is a big kid, not yet an adult.
There are two things that Kendrick loves.
His mom, Kristin.
And basketball.

Kristin has big plans for Kendrick.
He will not end up like me, she thinks.
I had no plans as a kid.
I did not finish school.
Kendrick will finish school.
Kendrick will go far!

There is one problem with Kristin's plan.
Kendrick does not intend to finish school.
In fact, Kendrick is not thinking of school at all.
He has big plans of his own.
Kendrick intends to drop out and become a basketball star.

Kristin has to admit:
Kendrick is fantastic at basketball.
He can sink the ball in the hoop from the other end of the court.
He can run faster than other kids.
He has fantastic skills on the court.

Kendrick's talent is dazzling.
He is electric when he has a basketball in his hands.
This kid has so much talent!
Everyone says that Kendrick will be a star.
He is quick and tall and strong, and he thinks fast.

But Kristin is still not impressed with Kendrick's skills
    in basketball.
She will admit that he has talent.
But talent with a basketball will not get you far!
"Kendrick," she says, "you must commit yourself to school.
You have to let go of this basketball stuff."

This is nuts to Kendrick.
"Ma," he says, "I am the best man on the team.
I am the number one front man.
I am quicker and stronger than all the other kids.
Coach Smith says I can get to the NBA!"

Kendrick is on the court all day long.
When school is finished, he grabs his basketball and runs to the
    court.
He is committed to basketball!
He knows he must work hard.
Getting better and stronger and faster—that is all that he thinks of.

Chapter Two

Kendrik has not told Kristin that he is getting an F in English.
When his teacher, Ms. Jensen, calls to tell her, Kristin hits the roof.
"YOU ARE OFF BASKETBALL!" she yells.
Kendrick is stunned.
He cannot exist with no basketball!

"Ma, you don't understand!" Kendrick yells.
"There is a man coming to watch the team
        next month!
He will pick two kids to go with him
        to a basketball clinic in Wisconsin!
The NBA reps will be at the clinic, picking kids to go
        to an NBA camp!
I have to be on the court when that man is watching!"

Kristin is not impressed.
"Son," she says, "tell me how many kids get picked
        for the NBA camps in the spring."
"A hundred! And I will be one of them!"
"And then tell me how many kids go to college?"
"I don't know," says Kendrick.
"Hundreds and hundreds. Hundreds of thousands.
Do you get this?" says Kristin.
"You are gambling to put all your eggs in that basket."

"The NBA is not a good prospect," says Kristin.
"College is the best prospect.
We are committed to you getting to college, and that is that.

No basketball until you stop letting basketball disrupt
    your commitment to school."
"But Ma!!!"
"No."

There is nothing left for Kendrick to do.
He must bring up his grades in English.
When he passes his pals on the basketball court,
    they yell to him.
"Come sink some hoops with us!
Come on, Kendrick! Man up!"
But Kendrick cannot stop.

Ms. Jensen assists Kendrick.
Kendrick sits in her class until 6 PM.
English was always difficult for Kendrick.
Math? No problem.
But English is difficult.
Ms. Jensen helps him.

Bit by bit, Kendrick's English skills have gotten better.
He is committed in his quest to pass English.
He does not get distracted.
He acts as if he is prepping for a big basketball game.
He thinks, *I must get stronger, faster, better.*
At the next exam, he is pumped up for it!

Kendrick is watching the basketball team.
He is on the bench.

All of a sudden, he sees Ms. Jensen running to him,
    with a test in her hand.
"Kendrick! This is your exam!
You passed!
You got a 92!"

Chapter Three

Kendrick is back on the basketball team.
All the kids are getting pumped for the big clinic.
A man from the Wisconsin Basketball Clinic will be watching.
He will pick two or three kids to go to the clinic,
    which lasts two weeks.
The kids who go to the clinic will be watched by reps
    from the NBA camp.
It is a big thing for a kid to get picked for this clinic.

Kendrick wants to get picked so bad.
But there is a problem.
When he was on the bench, prepping for his exam,
    another kid got his spot as the best front man.
This kid, Nelson, is now the best on the team.
Kendrick cannot stand Nelson!

Kendrick wants his spot back.
He wants to be the best.
But now Nelson is getting
    all the shots in.

He got all confident when Kendrick was gone.
"Hey man, too bad," says Nelson with a big grin.
He trots off, dribbling the ball.
Kendrick is so upset.

When Nelson gets the ball, Kendrick cannot get it back.
He cannot do the next jump.
He cannot run fast, or think quick.
He is in a fog.
Most of all, he has lost his boldness.
He is not at all confident.
He will not take a risk.

Coach Smith chats with Kendrick.
"What is the problem?" he says.
"Where is the old Kendrick?
Strong? Bold? Quick?
The kid who can sink a ball from the other end of the court?
What happened?"

"Coach, I've lost it," says Kendrick.
"I get it that Nelson is the best now."
Coach says, "Kendrick, you can't think of Nelson
     as an impediment.
Having talent next to you will push you up to the next level.
You two kids bring out the best in each other.
Nelson is your ticket to that clinic.
And you are his ticket."

At last, the old Kendrick is back!
He is confident and bold.
He is next to Nelson, and together they are dazzling.
They run the length of the court, dribbling, and then jump up
    to the basket next to each other, passing the ball back and forth.
The ball sinks into the basket.
Together, they are stars.

Chapter Four

This is it—the big match in which two kids will be picked to go
    to the Wisconsin Clinic.
Kendrick and Nelson are the two front men.
They pass the ball back and forth as if they have one mind.
The other team cannot stop them!
They sink the ball in the basket again and again and again.
In front of the stands, the man from the clinic is watching.
He is jotting things on his pad, and nodding and clapping.
When the match is finished, he nods to Kendrick and Nelson.
"You two," he says. "I want you two kids at the clinic!"

The clinic is the best thing that has ever happened to Kendrick.
He and Nelson are bunking together.
At the beginning of each day, they run to gulp down breakfast.
Then they go play basketball.
Back home, they were the stars.
At the clinic, all the kids are stars.
"You kids are all so talented," says one coach.

On the second day, the clinic hosts a chat about college.
"There are a hundred kids here," the coach says.
"Just two or three of you will go to the NBA camp.
But all of you are talented.
So what will you do with that talent if you don't get picked
    for the NBA camp?
You are all bold and quick. You have strength and commitment.
Think of what you can do with that boldness and that commitment.
It is not just for basketball."
Kendrick thinks, *The other kids should listen to this.*
But I am getting into the NBA!

The coach was right — having other talented kids with him
    is pushing Kendrick to the next level.
He is jumping and running and grabbing and dribbling
    as well as he can.
He has never given so much on the court.
He swings, he spins, he jumps, he sinks.
When the rep from the NBA camp is there, he goes even faster.

At the end of the clinic, all the kids are asked to sit on the benches.
The rep from the NBA camp spends a long time discussing
    the talent of all the kids.
"I wish I had spots for all of you," he says.
But just ten kids will get picked for this NBA camp.
He calls out ten kids, and they all get up, yelling and jumping
    with joy.
Kendrick is stunned. He was not called.
No NBA camp for Kendrick.
What?

Just Kendrick is left on the bench.
His head is in his hands.
"Hey kid! Number six!"
Kendrick lifts his head.
There is a man there who has watched the clinic.
"I'm Mac Jenkins. I'm a rep for several college basketball teams."
"Oh," says Kendrick. He is too depressed to respond.
"Kid, listen.
I want to bring you to another clinic.
It's not for the NBA. It's for college basketball."
"College basketball?" Kendrick thinks of his mom.
She would be thrilled to hear this.
"Yes.
You can get sent to college as a member of the basketball team."

Kendrick lets this sink in.
He thinks of himself at college.
Going to classes. Finishing college.
He thinks of himself as a college basketball player.
"OK," he says. "OK! YES!"

Patrick

Chapter One

This is Patrick.

Patrick is from the Dominican Republic.

But for the last 40 years, Patrick has lived in the USA.

Patrick has a wife, Janet, and three kids.

He has a job in a packing plant. He has had this job for 22 years.

He has lots of good benefits.

Patrick should be content.

In a few months, Patrick will be 65.

He will retire from his job.

His wife, Janet, says, "This will be fantastic, Patrick.

At last we can relax."

His son, Mitchell, says, "Dad, I predict you will love golf."

His son, Stefan, says, "Dad, you should be planning a big trip
    on a ship."

His daughter, Jennifer, says, "Dad, you can spend all the time
    you want fishing."

His grandchildren say, "Grandpop! We can go camping in Vermont!"

Patrick listens to everyone predict what will happen
    when his job ends.

He doesn't tell them yet, but he has other plans.

Patrick wants to go back to the Dominican Republic.

Many years back, Patrick's mom and dad did not last in the US.
They lasted just ten years, and then went back
    to the Dominican Republic.
But Patrick was an adult by then, and he had a good job,
    and a great gal.
He had just met Janet.
Janet and Patrick had a small wedding.
They wanted to be in the US.

Patrick visited his mom and dad
    often, with Janet
    and without Janet.
He went fishing with his dad.
And he went for coffee and
    empanadas with his mom.
"It's a good life in the Dominican
    Republic," his dad would say.
Patrick had to go back to the US for
    his job and his family.
But he would think, *Yes, it is*.
Patrick's mom and dad passed on.
He still misses them.

Patrick has been putting cash into the bank for the last 25 years.
He is thinking that he has enough cash to get a nice house
    in the Dominican Republic, so he can spend the rest of his life
    back home.
He just has to discuss his plan with his children.
He is a bit distressed, thinking of what they will all say.
He thinks there will be some conflict.

Patrick has called up his children and asked them to come to dinner.
The family sits on the deck.

Patrick is grilling chicken and eggplant on the grill.
The grandchildren are running in the back, and tossing and kicking
    a ball.
It is a fantastic setting, but Patrick is struggling to find the words
    to tell them his plan.
When dinner is finished, he taps his glass.
"I have something to tell you all," he says.
He winks at Janet. She does not wink back.

"I don't want to spend my next 20 years as an old man
    shoveling snow and struggling with the cold.
I am sick of the cold up here.
I want to go back to where I am from.
I want to go back to the Dominican Republic."
His kids just look at him with shock.
Janet says nothing.

Chapter Two

Patrick has told his family that he intends to go back
    to the Dominican Republic.
"I will spend my last years with my people," he says.
"At last, I'll be chatting in Spanish.
Having all the *empanadas* I want.
No more shoveling snow."
His family is stunned and shocked.

"What?! Dad, that is nuts!" his son Mitchell says at last.
"Dad, that is a bad, bad plan," his son Stefan says.
"Dad, what about the grandkids?" says his daughter Jennifer.
"They will never get to see you!"

Patrick can see that this will be difficult.
"Listen, he says, "I don't want you all telling me what to do.
For 40 years I have kept up with my job and my bills.
I have been a good dad.
Trumpet lessons. Band lessons. Acting class. Swimming class.
Soccer lessons. Getting you to chess club. And you to track."

Patrick goes on and on, listing all the things he has done
    for his kids.
It is a long list!
The kids cannot respond.
By the end, they are hanging their heads a bit.
"OK, Dad," says Stefan. "We get it. We get it!
You have done a lot for us.
But we will miss you if you go to the Dominican Republic."

"And what about Mom?
Mom, are you going to the Dominican Republic too?"
     Mitchell asks.
Janet says nothing.
Then, she shrugs.
"I am not sure. I think it will be difficult to adapt,
     but I am willing to attempt it."
Patrick puts his hand on her hand.
"Just think. No more shoveling snow!"
He adds, "And *empanadas*.
There is nothing like *empanadas* from the Dominican Republic."
Janet looks hesitant and not sure at all about this plan.

Patrick and Janet are on their way to the Dominican Republic.
They are just going to check it out.
Patrick is thrilled.
Janet is hesitant.
Janet's parents were Dominican, but she herself is
     an American citizen.
She has never been an immigrant.

"I know this will be a bit difficult for you," says Patrick.
"I was an immigrant in the US.
It is difficult to be in a new land.
But your Spanish is fantastic.
And I think you will love living in the Dominican Republic."

Janet is not so sure.
Yes, her Spanish is very good.
But Janet was born in the US.

When Janet was a kid, her grandma and grandpa chatted in Spanish.
Janet was good at Spanish.

A big part of Janet thinks this will be fantastic.
She can begin a new chapter in her life.
But she is hesitant as well.
She has never lived in a land other than the US.
What will this be like? Can she do it?
What if she can't?
Will she say good-bye to Patrick, after 30 years together?

Chapter Three

Janet and Patrick are in the Dominican Republic.
Patrick intends to spend the rest of his life here.
He is finished with his job.
It is his turn to sit back and relax!

But his wife, Janet, is not so sure.
They are spending a month here to check it out.
If it is OK with Janet, they will go back to the US just to get their
    stuff and sell their house.
Janet is expecting that it will be difficult to adapt to this new life.

"Hon!" Patrick grabs her hand and brings her to a food stand.
"*Empanadas*! The Dominican kind!"
Empanadas are a snack. They consist of a tender crust
    folded over a filling, such as chicken or meat.

Patrick puts an *empanada* into a napkin and hands it to Janet.
"They call them *pastelitos* here," he says.
"I never could find the exact same thing in the US."
Janet is nibbling on the tender crust of her chicken *pastelito*.
"Mmm," she says.

"Is this not the best snack you ever had?"
Janet has to admit, Dominican *empanadas* are fantastic!
She is picking up the remnants from her napkin,
    getting every last bit.
"These bring me back to when I was a kid," says Patrick.

The *empanadas* are fantastic,
    but Janet is having a
    difficult adjustment.
Patrick is running all over,
    finding old pals.
He has gone fishing.
He has gone swimming.
He has gone golfing.
But Janet does not want
    to fish or swim or golf.
She wants a pal to chat with.

Janet is sick of how hot it is in the Dominican Republic.
She is sick of how different it is here.
She is sick of struggling to adapt.
She is sick of the fact that she has no pals.
She just sits all day and does nothing.

"Patrick," she says, "I don't think this is going to work."

"What?" Patrick looks crestfallen.

"I have no one to chat with.

I do not want to go fishing or golfing or swimming.

In the US, I was busy planning events, and chatting with pals.

Here, I have nothing to do."

Patrick feels panicked.

All his plans will be finished if Janet thinks
    the Dominican Republic is not for her.

How could he have forgotten to help her find some pals?

He was so distracted by his own fun.

So now Patrick is calling all his pals.

"Let's have a party," he says.

"Bring your wife!"

Chapter Four

Janet has discovered a pack of pals.

In the morning, she gets together with them.

They go jogging, and then they go for coffee.

Bev is her best pal.

Bev is from the US, but has a Dominican husband, just like Janet.

"I hit the jackpot with Bev," says Janet. "What a fantastic pal."

Bev and Janet chat in Spanish and in English.

They both have grandkids.

They have plans to host their grandkids at the same time,
    so the grandkids can be pals, too.

Patrick and Janet are content.
They have sold their house in the US.
They are living in a rental apartment.
They are loving living in the Dominican Republic!
Now they just have to get their kids and grandkids to visit.
That could be a problem.

The grandchildren are off school at the end of winter.
Mitchell, Stefan, and Jennifer plan to visit with their parents.
They are conflicted about this.
They do not want to have a good time!
They intend to push their parents to come back to the US.

The first day of the trip, all the grandchildren get a bad sunburn.
The second day of the trip, Mitchell gets sick and has to go to bed
    for the rest of the day.
The third day of the trip, Jennifer's oldest child has to go
    to the hospital for stitches.
The fourth day of the trip, Stefan and Mitchell get into
    a big conflict about who will pay for dinner.
They are yelling at each other in the restaurant.
"Hmm," says Janet, "I'm not sure all the kids visiting
    at the same time was a good plan."

On the sixth day, Patrick takes all the grandkids fishing.
The moms and dads have a picnic with Janet.
Jennifer wants to have a chat.
"Mom, when do you think you and Dad will come back
    to the US?"

Janet looks shocked.
"Come back? What? No! We are very content here.
Your dad has his fishing and his garden.
I have my pals.
I love it here."
Jennifer looks conflicted.

On the seventh day, Patrick takes all the grandkids
    to get *empanadas* at the stand in the park.
"Kids," he says, "these bring me back to when I was a kid.
You kids are all 50% Dominican.
This is part of your ethnic heritage."
Patrick says all this in Spanish.
He is all Spanish, all the time now.
The kids understand him.

Patrick hands an *empanada* in a napkin to each kid.
The kids are hesitant.
But soon they are nibbling the tender crusts
    and munching on the snack.
"Yum!" say the smallest grandkid. "Can I have another?"
He says this in Spanish.
Patrick is full of happiness and contentment.

When Patrick and the grandkids get back from the *empanada* trip,
    the moms and dads are all relaxing in the sun.
They have been shopping and swimming and relaxing all day.
The kids rush in, chatting about the *empanadas*, in Spanish.
They have packed *empanadas* to share with their moms and dads.
"You got them to use their Spanish?" asks Mitchell, shocked.

"Papa!" says Mitchell's smallest kid.
"When can we come back to the Dominican Republic?"
He says this in perfect Spanish.
Janet and Patrick wink at each other.
It's going to be OK.

Isabel

Chapter One

This is Isabel.
Isabel is a resident of Manhattan.
Isabel is from Brazil.
Isabel has a job as a consultant
    for a laptop company.
All is well with Isabel, but something is
    about to happen that will upset her life.

"Hello, Isabel!"
It is Isabel's mother calling from Brazil.
"Hello, Mother," says Isabel.
"Isabel," says her mother, "I have such a grand thing to tell you."
"Yes, Mother?" says Isabel.
"I want to live in Manhattan!"

This is a shock to Isabel.
Isabel's mother is still in Brazil.
She is from the old world.
Isabel does not think that she is a good fit for Manhattan.

"Mother. What? Why do you want to do this?
It is not easy to be in Manhattan.

It is fast and big.
Mother, I do *not* think this is a good plan.
Mother, I do *not* think you will fit in here."

But Isabel's mother will not let go of this fantastic plan.
"I am so sick of Brazil!" she says.
"Too much gossip! All my pals just gossip all the time.
It is too small here.
I want a fresh start."

Isabel feels a bit sick.
Just think: her mother in Manhattan!
Living with Isabel!
Isabel is independent.
She has her job, and her pals, and her fantastic apartment.
Her mother will not fit into this life.

Isabel's mother still dresses as if it is 50 years past.
She dresses in stockings and heels, and black dresses.
She goes to mass on Sundays.
She does not drink or go out at night.
She will expect Isabel to dress like this, and to act like this.

Oh my God, thinks Isabel.
What am I going to do?
She cannot expect me to live like I am still in Brazil, and it is 1950.
But to her mother she says, "OK, Mother.
I will pick you up at the airport."

Chapter Two

Isabel's mother did not like the lunch on the plane.
And the airline lost two of her bags.
And she did not like the cab.
And she did not like the fact that the sun was hidden by clouds.
But at last Isabel and her mother get to Isabel's apartment.
The cab has left them with Isabel's mother's six bags.
Isabel's mother gasps.
"You are on the *fifth* floor?!" she says.

Isabel has a fantastic apartment.
It is small. It has one bed, and a living room, and a kitchen.
The bathroom has a pink tub and sink.
"Look, Mother," she says.
"You can see the Hudson River from the bathroom!"
Isabel's mother sits in a slump in the kitchen.
"The air is bad here," she says.

Isabel brings her mother to Aspen Street to check out the shops.
"Look, Mother," says Isabel.
"We can eat in a Mexican restaurant, or Indian, or Chinese.
And I love how, on this street, you can see people from all over.
The mix of people is terrific! And all the food! It's fantastic, no?"
Isabel's mother does not think so.
"Hmph," she says. "Nothing from Brazil?"

On Monday, Isabel has to go to her job.
"Mother, will you be OK?
I must go to my job. But I will be back at 6.

Then we can have dinner at the Mexican restaurant. OK?"
Isabel's mother says, "Yes, I will be OK.
Do not think about me. I will see you at 6."
"OK!" says Isabel.
"But just today, yes?" says her mother.

"Mother," says Isabel, "I go to my job on Monday, Tuesday,
    Wednesday, Thursday, and Friday."
Isabel's mother is in shock.
"Five days?!"
"Yes, Mother. Five days.
I must have a job so I can pay my rent."
Her mother is still in shock.
"But what kind of life is this?" she asks.
"How can you find a husband like this?"

Isabel shuts her eyes.
"Mother," she says.
"I am not hunting for a husband.
I want to do well at my job.
For now, that is my biggest interest."
Isabel's mother goes very still.
"And Mother? I must work a lot.
That is what it is like in Manhattan.
Rent and food are expensive.
It is just how it is here in Manhattan."

For a long moment, nothing is said.
At last, Isabel's mother says,
"OK. That is OK.

I understand that you must go to your job a lot.
But there is one problem with that."
"Yes?" said Isabel.
"Well," her mother says, "what do you expect me to do all day?"

Isabel has to stop herself.
She would have liked to yell, "I did not think you should
    come here!
I told you that Manhattan was not a good fit for you!"
But she cannot yell at her mother.
So she says, "Well, Mother, you could get a job."
Or you could find some other women from Brazil.
You could go to the park all day.
But there is one thing, Mother, that you must do."
"Yes, love?" asks her mother.
"You must let me go to my job!"
Isabel slams the door and leaves.

Chapter Three

Isabel's mother has adjusted to Manhattan.
She lets Isabel go to her job.
She has gotten accustomed to the air in Manhattan,
She has gotten accustomed to Isabel's small apartment.
She has discovered that Mexican food is wonderful!
She will call Isabel at the job and say, "Let's get Mexican tonight!"

She is much better.
She likes Manhattan.

But there is one thing.
"Isabel," she says.
"It is wonderful here
    in Manhattan.
You have a good job.
    You have a
    fantastic apartment.
But there is still one
    big thing you are
    missing."

"What is that, Mother?" asks Isabel.
"A husband, of course!"

"Mother . . ."
"Isabel, a husband is important.
You must find a husband.
Did you even begin to look?
Isabel, I watch you go out, and you do not look your best.
You must get dressed up all the time.
You never know when you will find your husband.
If you are dressed like a slob, how he will find you?"

"Mother . . ."
"Isabel, this is important.
I think I must help you with this.
If I do not help you, it could be that you never find a husband.
And then I will not get a grandchild.
So, I will find your husband for you."
"Mother!"
"Now, now, Isabel. No fussing.
I will find you a husband, and that is that.

I can tell that you need my help."
With that, Isabel's mother gets her jacket and her bag
     and leaves the apartment.
Isabel is stunned and shocked.

Isabel calls her pal Meg.
"Can we get a drink?" she says.
"I have almost lost my mind."
"Yes," says Meg. "But what is the problem?"
"My mother!" says Isabel.
"She is living in my apartment.
She is controlling my life.
And now, she is out looking for a husband for me!"
"Oh God. Let's go now!" says Meg.

Isabel finds Meg at a bar on West End Street.
"OK," says Meg. "Get a drink. And then tell me everything."
"It's my mother," says Isabel.
"She thinks she must find me a husband.
Why did this happen?
My life was OK when she was in Brazil."
"Well," says Meg. "I think she needs something to do.
Can she get a job?"
"My mother is from a different time," says Isabel.
"She never had a job."
"OK," says Meg. "Could she find a job that is not for cash?
Like with children?
Or with old people?
Or sick people?"
"Hmm," says Isabel.
"That could be . . ."

Isabel is out on the hunt for a job for her mother.
Her mother is out on the hunt for a husband for Isabel.
Isabel checks the hospital and the library.
"Hello, do you have a spot for a woman who wants to help?"
Her mother checks the bank and the library.
"Hello!" she says, to men she thinks look rich.

Isabel gets back home to find her mother humming
    and singing to herself.
"Hello, Kitten," she says to Isabel.
Kitten is Isabel's nickname from when she was a small child.
"Hi, Mother," says Isabel. "What is getting you all glad like this?"
"I have planned a big event for us," says her mother.
She has a big grin on her face.
"Well, that is interesting," says Isabel.
"I have a planned a big event for us as well."
They are both grinning and full of plans.

Chapter Four

Isabel's mother has set Isabel up with a man.
Isabel goes to the address her mother has given her.
It is a nice Mexican spot.
There is her mother, sitting with a man.
"Isabel! This is Mr. Griffin.
He is in banking. He is very elegant, no?"
And to Mr. Griffin, she says, "This is my daughter, Isabel.
She is just finished with her job. She is stunning, no?"
Mr. Griffin grasps Isabel's hands.
"I am thrilled to meet the child of such a fantastic woman."

He is still grinning
    at Isabel's mother.
His gray hair is slicked back.
He is elegant.
But a bit old for Isabel.

"Mother, can we have a chat?"
Isabel gets up and beckons to her mother.
"In the women's room?"
Isabel and her mother go across the restaurant
    to the women's room.
"Mother! Are you kidding? He's too old for me!"
"Oh Isabel," says her mother. "Hush, Kitten!
Do not have such a small mind.
He's so elegant and charming!"

It is the next day.
"Mother, I want you to go check out the hospital.
I understand they need volunteers."
"What is a volunteer?"
"It is when you work for free, just to help."
Isabel's mother scoffs at this, but goes along with Isabel.

She does not like the hospital.
"Too much sickness here!" she whispers to Isabel. "The air is bad."
As they are exiting, Isabel spots a Help Wanted ad.
She grabs the ad on the way out.

"Isabel, have you called Mr. Griffin?"
"Mother, I told you he is much too old for me."

"But so elegant! And he is not old! You must consider him, Isabel."
"Mother, I am not at all interested in him.
And the other thing about him, Mother, is that . . .
I think he is interested in you."
"What?" Isabel's mother blushes.
"No! Really? You think so?"
All of a sudden, Isabel's mother can't stop giggling.

Isabel has sent in an application for the job at the hospital.
She gets a call.
"Hello, Isabel Alvez?"
"Yes, this is Isabel Alvez."
"I am calling from the hospital, about the job.
You are the applicant we are most interested in.
Can you come in to discuss the job with us?"
"Yes!"

The director of the hospital staff is discussing the job with Isabel.
"You would be the boss of the help desk," he says.
The boss! This is what Isabel has always wanted.
"You will have to be at the hospital until seven PM.
And you will be on call," said the director.
Then Isabel's heart sinks.

She cannot be at the job that much.
She cannot do that to her mother.
Isabel exits the hospital with a sinking feeling.

When she gets to the apartment, she expects her mother to be upset.
She has been out for a long time.

But her mother is not there!
Isabel fixes herself dinner, and watches TV.

Her mother gets home at ten. She is giggling and grinning.
"Oh, that Mr. Griffin," she says, blushing like mad.
Hmm, maybe her mother would not mind Isabel having long hours
    at the job!

It is six months later.
Isabel has started her new job. She loves it.
She works long hours.
After work, sometimes she meets her mother and Mr. Griffin
    at the Mexican restaurant.
They are in love.
"You know, Isabel," says her mother.
"I always knew living in the US would be a good thing!"
Isabel just grins and nods.
She is happy. And her mother is happy.
All is good.

Bethann

Chapter One

This is Bethann.
She is 65.
Bethann's husband passed on seven years ago.
Her children are big, and are living far away.
Bethann is all finished with her job. She is all by herself.
She thinks a lot about her home, Trinidad.

When she was a child in Trinidad, Bethann had a big family.
She had her mom and dad, her aunts and uncles, her cousins,
    and her siblings.
She had her grandmother and, best of all, she had her granddad.
She used to help her granddad in his garden.
They planted all kinds of things in the garden.
They planted radishes, squash, eggplant, and more.
Bethann loved helping her granddad in the garden.

Now she is old, and her granddad passed on a long, long time ago.
There is not much left in Trinidad for Bethann.
She cannot go back to Trinidad, but she thinks about Trinidad
    all day long.
One day, thinking about Trinidad, she can almost smell the flowers
    and the garden from back home.
She can smell the tropics!

The scent of the tropics engulfs her.
It is intoxicating!

A tropical scent has come into her apartment.
That fantastic tropical scent of flowers, and Trinidad,
    and her granddad, and herself as a child with a big family.
Bethann looks out the window, squinting in the sun.
At the end of her street, she spots a splash of pink and red.
Someone has planted a rose bush, and a pot of hibiscus.
Someone has planted flowers and bushes.
These pink and red splashes of color, and this fantastic smell
    of the tropics, are like sweet kisses from Bethann's past.

Well, that is it.
Bethann must get some pots of flowers and bushes and hibiscus
    for herself!
But there is a problem: Bethann has no front stoop.
She thinks, *Where will I put those flowers and the bushes?*
Mulling this over, she finds herself staring across the street.
There is a kid in the lot. He is hitting a ball at the wall.
There is nothing in the lot. It is vacant, empty.
Could Bethann plant things in the vacant lot?

Bethann is at the shop across the street.
"Hello, I would like to find out whose lot that is."
"That vacant lot?" the man says. "That lot belongs to the city."
"The city?"
"Yes, and they do nothing with it.
It is a spot for dumping. People put scraps and junk in there."
Hmm, thinks Bethann. *I must go to City Hall.*
That kid from the lot is watching Bethann.

Bethann is at City Hall.
She is with Ms. Minton, the woman who monitors
    the development of vacant lots in the city.
"I want to plant a garden," Bethann says.
"Well," says Ms. Minton. "You must have a lot of commitment
    from the people on the block.
You must get 100 signatures."
"I can get that," says Bethann.
Ms. Minton squints at Bethan through her glasses. "You think so?"
"I know so," says Bethann.
(She doesn't know this! But she just says it.)
"Hmm. Well. If you can gather one hundred signatures,
    the city will let you put a garden into the lot."
With that, Ms. Minton turns her back on Bethann
    and gets back to work.

Bethann thinks it will be difficult to get 100 signatures.
But it is not difficult.
She stands in front of the lot, telling people about the garden.
All of them sign their names.
The kid from the lot helps her.
He stands next to Bethann, yelling, "Do you want a garden?
Sign up here, people!"
All the people are interested in the garden.
A lot of them had gardens back home, just like Bethann.
At the end of the day, she calls Ms. Minton, the woman
    from City Hall.
"Ms. Minton? I have the signatures. Come and get them!
And bring some shovels!"

Chapter Two

Bethann did not think so many people on the block
    would want to help with this project.
This is what they are telling her:
"I miss the garden I had back home."
"The radishes and tomatoes in the shop are disgusting!
    I want them fresh from the garden!"
"When I was small, my mom and I would plant things.
    I miss that. I want to do it again."
"I want my kids to plant things.
    They think the only way to find food is to go shopping."
Beth tells them, "See you at the planning meeting!"

Ms. Minton has a big list of things they must do.
"The first thing is to test the soil," she says.
At the next planning meeting, Ms. Minton is there.
She almost seems glad to tell Bethann and all the people:
"I'm sorry, but we ran tests on the soil in the lot,
    and there are metal remnants in the soil.
You cannot plant a garden with metal in the soil."
Everyone is stunned and sad.
Just like that, the project is finished.
Or is it?

The kid puts up his hand.
He has to jump up and down, and still no one calls on him.
At last, he yells out, "Why can't we plant in boxes?"
For a second, no one says a thing.
Then . . . "Yes!" "Boxes!" "The kid is right!"
Ms. Minton pinches up her lips.

She squints at her papers, shuffling them around, and then, at last,
she shrugs and nods.
"OK," Bethann calls out. "The project is back on!"

This is how the people get the cash to construct the garden boxes:
They go back to City Hall to ask for funding.
They send the kids to shops to ask for cash.
The kids say, "We will put your name on a big post in the garden,
saying 'Thanks to our sponsors!'"
A garden shop offers to bring soil in a big dump truck.
They get a grant from a big box shop.
A big lumber shop offers to bring lumber.
It is all coming together!

Today is the day to construct the boxes.
All day the men and women work hard together, cutting wood
and constructing boxes.
The kids are running and yelling and having fun.
A man from Elm Street, Mel, has set up a grill.
Everyone brings things for the grill.
A kid with a basketball, Kendrick, has plugged in his iPod
and is blasting music.
This is what it was like in Trinidad, thinks Bethann.
So many people, so much music, so much fun . . .
There is still something missing, but she can't think what it is.

The next day is planting day!
All day, people are planting seeds and transplanting pots of flowers
into the garden boxes.
Bethann has a box all for herself.

She plants all the things she remembers planting with her granddad.
"Well, well, well," says Ms. Minton.
She has come to see the garden.
Bethann stands up. "Did you see?
Did you see this fantastic garden?"
Ms. Minton pinches her lips and
    squints in the sun.
"I must admit, you did it."
Bethann nods and grins.
Something is still missing.
But she is glad this garden is up and running!

All through that spring and summer, the garden prospers.
The plants and flowers are coming up.
Bethann has set up a sitting spot.
The grill is still there.
The garden is a spot for people on the block to stop in
    and hang out.
They check on the plants.
They chat.
They plant more stuff.
They grill hot dogs.
All the people on the street are connecting with each other.
Bethann is so glad.

One day, Bethann is sitting in the garden.
An old man calls to her.
"Lady, you are still missing something from your garden."
Bethann thinks something is still missing,
    but she does not know what.

Does this man have it?
He holds out a box for Bethann to see.
Two chickens are in the box, pecking and clucking.
"Can't have a garden with no chickens, lady."

Chapter Three

Chickens are not what Bethann had in mind!
But the man is insistent.
"Lady," he says, "a garden must have chickens.
The chickens eat scraps, and you can make a compost
    with their dung."
"What's a compost?" asks Bethann.
"It's a box of scraps.
You gather all the scraps from the kitchen,
    like the tops of radishes, or egg shells.
You add chicken dung.
You put it all together and mix it up and let it rot.
Then it's the best soil, to put back in the garden."

But there is no spot to put chickens.
"Mister, that sounds great, but I don't think we can have chickens
    in this garden."
"Why not?" The kid says this.
The kid who is always in the garden.
Bethann says to him, "Well, we have no chicken coop."
"Miss Bethann, if we can put up a garden in a vacant lot,
    we can put a chicken coop together."

The kid is holding one of the chickens and petting it.
"I never held a chicken," he says.

Mel, from the next block, says he
    will put together a chicken
    coop.
"But I want some eggs,"
    he says, grinning.
There is still lumber in the lot,
    left from the garden boxes.
It is a quick project to put together
    a small chicken coop and a pen.
Within a few days, the chickens are penned in and content.
The compost is up and running.
The chickens are fun to watch.

All is well in the garden.
The plants are coming along.
Flowers are blossoming.
Radishes are coming up.
Plants are getting tall and full.
The chickens are scratching and pecking in the pen.
The kids get to hold the hens.
They bring the eggs back to their moms and dads.

"Miss Bethann! Miss Bethann!"
It is not 6 AM yet, and Bethann is still in bed.
The kid from the garden is yelling to her.
She rushes to the window. "What is it?"
"The chickens are not in the pen! They were kidnapped!"

"Kidnapped? Who would kidnap a chicken?

Hold on. Just let me get dressed."

Bethann rushes to get dressed, and then rushes to the garden.

The kid is so upset. He is almost sobbing.

"We have to get those chickens back!"

Bethann looks at the kid, and something in her chest melts.

She wants to grab this kid and give him the biggest hug.

But she just pats him on the hand.

"We will find those chickens," she says.

The kid is obsessed with finding the chickens.

"We are missing two chickens," he says to everyone he passes.

Bethann brings brushes and paint to the garden.

"Let's put up a big sign about these missing chickens," she says.

She gets a brush wet with paint, and writes, "MISSING HENS.

    HELP BRING THEM BACK!"

A man and woman are grilling. They put fresh chicken on the grill.

The kid gasps. "Chicken!" he says in a hushed voice.

He nods at the man and looks at Bethann.

Bethann grins and shushes him.

"Miss Bethann, did you call the cops?"

The cops? Bethann has not considered this.

When the cops get to the garden, Bethann discovers that cops

    do not think missing chickens are a big problem.

One cop is examining the garden boxes with interest.

"I had a garden when I was a kid," he says.

"We planted squash and pumpkins.

Are you planting squash and pumpkins?

Our squash and pumpkins were fantastic.

My mom would put them in pies . . ."

The other cop is examining the chicken coop.
"*Chickens?* In the *city?*
When I was a kid we had chickens. The best eggs!
You cannot get eggs like that in the city.
Well, well, well. Chickens in the city . . ."

"Yes," says Bethann, "It is wonderful having chickens in the city.
But not when they get kidnapped!
You must help us find them."
"Miss Bethann?" It is the kid. He is tugging on the hem
    of Bethann's dress. "Miss Bethann? Miss Bethann!"
"Yes, what is it?"
"That lady is back. With the glasses. From the city."
Bethann looks past the cops. Ms. Minton is there.
"I'm sorry, Bethann," she says. "The city wants this lot back.
They want to put up a development.
We are shutting this garden."

Chapter Four

"There is nothing I can do," Ms. Minton says.
"The city wants to develop your block.
They will be fixing the streets, and investing in your block.
You should be glad."
Bethann is shocked. "You cannot do this to us," she says.
"It's not me. It's the city. And there is nothing that can be done.
You will need to find a new spot to have your garden.
You have 30 days to give up the lot."
And with that, Ms. Minton is gone.

"Miss Bethann," says the kid. "You can't let them do that."
"Don't you fret," says Bethann. "I will not let them."
"What are you going to do?"
"I just need to put together a plan."
"I will help."
"I know you will, baby."

Bethann has no plan.
She calls for a meeting to tell what is happening.
Everyone is shocked.
"How can they do that?"
"That is so unjust!"
"We send in our taxes! This is our block!"
"This is an attack on us!"
"I know, I know," says Bethann. "It is unjust.
But what should we do?"
"Let's push back!"
Mel stands up. "This is what we should do," he says.
"We push back, the democratic way.
We tell the newspapers.
We call our congressmen.
We pack the meetings at City Hall."
And as they discuss the problem, everyone gets more and more
    committed to fixing this problem.
"We will win this," says Bethann.

Step One is to tell everyone.
"There is strength in numbers," says Bethann.
"We must get everyone who loves the garden to help us."
The brushes and paint are back, for the signs.
The signs say things like, "Don't mess up the garden."

"Gardens are good for children and other living things."
"SAVE THE GARDEN!"
As people pass the garden, they stop to ask what is happening.
"The garden is beautiful," they say.
"Why do they want to mess it up?"
They are told, "Please come to the City Hall meeting
    on September fifth."
And, "Please send this letter to the Senator.
And call the district's planning group.
Tell them the garden is a good thing."

The next step is to tell the newspapers.
Bethann pens a letter:
    "Dear Editors, On my block, we have put together a fantastic
    garden. We got a grant from the city, and we put together the
    Aspen Street Garden. This is a wonderful gathering spot for our
    block. Now the city wants the lot back. Please help us tell the city
    that this is unjust, after all the work we have put into this lot.
    Thank you. Best, Bethann Jackson, 68 Aspen Street."

Three days later, she gets a call.
"Hello, Ms. Bethann Jackson? This is Fred Jenkins.
I am an editor at the newspaper. I got your letter.
I want to visit the garden."

The next step is to call up the political bigwigs.
Bethann and all the men and women call their district's
    congressman to ask for help.
And one day . . . a man visits the garden.
He is well dressed, and has a woman with him snapping pictures.

"Hello, Miss Bethann!"
He is confident and charming, with a big, warm grin.
He extends his hand to Bethann, and grins for a picture.
"I am Congressman Benjamin Smith.
This is my assistant, Janet Smalls.
We have come to see the garden."
"At last!" says Bethann. "We have been calling and calling you!"
"Yes, I know! I have gotten 162 calls about your garden!
That is a lot of calls!
When I hear from that number of people in my district,
    I come see what is happening."

The last step in the plan is to pack the September planning meeting.
The district holds this meeting at City Hall.
The room is full! There is no spot left for sitting.

The meeting begins.
There are random subjects to address, such as:

The missing street sign at the end of Ash Street.
The dumpster next to the big box shop, which is attracting rats.
The stop light that is blinking at the crossing by Aspen Street.
At last, the topic is the garden.
Bethann gets up and stands at the front of the hall.
She is trembling.
"The Aspen Street Garden is a fantastic thing," she begins.
She tells all about how the garden was put together
    and how wonderful it is for everyone on the block.

Then Ms. Minton stands up.
"There is nothing we can do about this," she says.
"The city wants the lot back."
Everyone is yelling. "This is our block!" "This is unjust!"

A door slams at the back of the hall.
It is Congressman Benjamin Smith.
"Hello!" he calls to the people, flashing his big grin.
"Hello! I am here to chat about the garden."
Ms. Minton says, "Thank you for coming, Congressman.
But I am sad to say that there is nothing we can do."

"Ms. Minton," the congressman scolds, "there is *always* something
    we can do.
When I get 175 . . ."
The congressman's assistant stops him and whispers to him.
"Oh," he says. "The number keeps getting bigger!
When I get *195* letters and calls from the public about a problem
    on one block, I think we can find something to do."
The people are hushed, listening.

"I have gotten funding from a non-profit called the Public Land Trust.
They have said they will help to buy this lot from the city.
You will still have to find the rest of the funding by next spring,
    but the bulk of the cost will be given by the PLT."
Congressman Smith stops for a second, and stares out at everyone
    in the hall.
Then he yells with his big grin flashing, "Let's save this garden!"

Everyone is standing and yelling.
Fists are pumping in the air.
Feet are stomping.
Hands are clapping.
No one is yelling and clapping more than the kid and Bethann.

It is September, time for a Harvest Fest.
The grill is on. Kendrick's iPod is blasting.
Children are running and yelling.
Bethann and the kid are sitting together, having hot dogs and salad.
All of a sudden she knows what is missing from the garden.

"Do you have a garden box?" she asks the kid.
"No, Miss Bethann, I just watch other people planting."
"Well, why don't you help me? I could use your help.
We could do that box together."

"Yes, Miss Bethann. I want to help."
Bethann hugs him.
"That's what's been missing from this garden!" she says.
"I must have a friend to help me tend these plants."

All of a sudden, the kid gasps. "What's that?"
The cops are coming in, with two chickens in their arms.
"We got your chickens back!" they say.
"When we read about the garden getting saved, we said,
      'We got to find those chickens!'"
Bethann grins and shrugs.
"Well, next problem, you can help us faster, OK?
You men want some hot dogs?"

Bethann and the kid sit in the garden, with the hens back in their
      pen, and the music blasting, and the food and drinks coming.
And they spend the whole long day together like that.

Will Bethann and all the men and women of Aspen Street
      get the rest of the funds for the garden?
Read to the end of Level 4 to find out!

Level 4
Pine Street

The Men and Women of Pine Street

Rose — a woman who bakes cakes
James — a man who came to the US from Rome
June — a woman who wants to get back with her children
Mike — a man who has to take care of his sick mom
Miles — a kid who hides a lost dog
Jane — a woman who figures out how to save a garden

Rose

Chapter One

This is Rose.
Rose has just come to the US.
She is from Haiti.
Her English is not perfect,
    but it is fine.

Rose wants to make it in the US!
She plans to make it big.
When she was a kid, her nickname was Wild Rose.
No one could ever tame this Rose.

Rose goes out to find a job.
She has a bad time.
She goes to a restaurant, a hospital, and a book store.
At all of these spots, it is the same.

"Do you have a high school diploma?" they ask.
Each spot asks Rose the same thing.
Rose does not have a high school diploma.
She went to school for just nine years.

But she is quick and smart.
Rose knows English because of American songs.
As a kid, she would chat in English to anyone she could find.
Now her English is fine.

But all the bosses want a high school diploma.
They do not care if you are quick and smart.
"Sorry," they say.
"You must finish high school."

You cannot tame a wild rose.
And you cannot tame this Rose.
Rose does not have time to finish high school.
She must make money now!

Rose sits in her sister June's home, and has a bite of black cake.
Black cake is a fantastic thing that is made all through the islands.
Rose learned how to make it from an aunt in Trinidad.
She always made these cakes so well.
"If only you could sell these cakes!" says June.

Chapter Two

Now Rose has a plan!
She will sell her black cakes.
A black cake is a common thing in the West Indies,
    where Rose is from.
It is based on the old British spice cakes.
But the West Indians made the cake their own.
A black cake has rum and lots of spices in it.
The cakes have to cure for months.

Rose cannot take months to let the cakes cure.
"This is America," she says.
"I will make a new kind of black cake.
I will invent a *quick* black cake."
She spends time inventing this cake.
At last she has it.

"How did you make this cake so fast?" asks June.
"Black cake takes months!"
But Rose will not tell.
"It tastes the same, right?" she says.
June nods. "It tastes like home," she says with a wistful tone.
"It makes me think of our Auntie from Trinidad."

Rose will call her cakes "Rose's Black Cakes, A TASTE OF HOME."
June was always good at art.
She makes a logo for Rose to use for her cakes.
It is beautiful!
Rose makes copies and cuts the card to attach to her cakes.

Rose is all set. She has lots of cakes!
She sets up her cakes on the sidewalk.
She puts up a big, beautiful sign.
"Rose's Black Cake. A TASTE OF HOME!"
She calls out to people as they pass.

"Don't you miss black cake from home?" she calls.
Rose has no shame. She is not timid.
This is the fun part for her.
She gets to call out to people and wink and chat and have fun.
And she gets to sell her fantastic cakes and make lots of cash!

A man stops to get a bite of cake.
"Make it a good size," he says.
"I have not had black cake in so long."
He takes a bite. He shuts his eyes and smiles.
"MMMMM," he says.
"This is the best black cake!" he says.

Rose's cake business is getting so big!
People love her cakes!
"Can you make coffee, too?" they ask.
So she makes coffee and sells that, too.
People stop on their way home from the job.
Some people take an entire cake.
It is all good until one day, when Rose gets a visit from the cops.

Chapter Three

"Lady," says the cop, "this is not OK.
You can't just set up a store on the sidewalk."
Rose did not know this.
"You can't?"
"No way," says the cop. "We could fine you hundreds of dollars!"
"Please do not fine me," says Rose. "How can I make this OK?"
"You must go to City Hall and get a permit."
"OK! OK!" says Rose. "I will do that. Thank you."

Rose's next stop is City Hall.
"I would like to get a permit to sell my cakes on the street,"
    she says.
"OK," says the lady. "But first you must get a license to sell food.
Go to that line over there."
Rose goes to that line.
"I would like to get a license to sell food," she says.
"So that I can get a permit to sell my cakes on the street."
"OK," says the man, "but first you must get a tax ID number.
Go to that line over there."

Rose has gotten her tax ID number.
Rose has gotten her license to sell food.
And now Rose is back in line to get the permit.
She has her forms filled out. She has her check to pay the costs.
She thinks she is all set.

The lady takes her forms and her check.
"OK, hon. Thanks. We will let you know."
"What? What do you mean? How long will that take?"
The lady shrugs. "It takes a long time.
There is a long line of applicants.
It could take months for us to grant you the permit."

You cannot tame a wild rose.
And you cannot tame this Rose.
But you can tire her out until she cannot cope.
Rose is tired.

When Rose is tired, she bakes cakes.
She goes back to her sister's home, and bakes cakes.
Lots of cakes.
"Rose! What are you doing?" yells her sister.
"How will you sell these cakes?"

Rose stops to think.
"I will sell them, one way or another," she says.
She packs up a cake in a box, and makes it look pretty.
She takes it with her and hits the street to find a bake shop.
She will sell these cakes in a bake shop, instead of on the street.

Her first stop is a coffee shop called the Trinidad Shop.
The owner of the shop is skeptical.
"There is no black cake like my mama's cake," he says.
But he takes a bite of cake.
"Oh. Oh wow. Oh man. *Mama*!" he shouts.
His tiny old mama comes shuffling out from the back.
"Mama, taste this cake," says the man.
His tiny old mama tastes the cake. She thinks for a bit.
She looks at her son.
"Son," she says, "we must sell these cakes."

Chapter Four

"Rose's Black Cake: A TASTE OF HOME!"
Rose's cake is now sold in a handful of stores and shops.
People love the taste of the cake.
And Rose keeps on expanding.

One day she goes to a shop on the other side of the city.
It is a posh district.
A pal told her there is an upscale shop that sells things
    from all over the globe.
"I would like to offer my cakes for you to sell,"
    she says to the owner.
"This is a black cake.
It is an old kind of cake from my part of the world.
It is much loved by people from these parts.
The taste might be odd at first, but then you will come to love it!"

The man in the shop tastes the cake.
"Wow," he says. "That is a fantastic cake.
I like that it is made by you, not by a big bake shop
  hundreds of miles from here."
Rose smiles. "Thank you," she says.
"But one thing," the man says.
"Do you have a permit to sell these cakes?"
"A permit?" Rose is stunned.
"No one has asked me for a permit to sell to shops."
The man shakes his head. "If you do not have a permit,
  you must bake the cakes in a kitchen that has a license."

Oh no.
Rose shakes her head.
"I don't bake them in a licensed kitchen," she says.
"I bake them at home."
The man thinks.
"I would like to sell these cakes," he says.
"If you can find a licensed kitchen that will let you bake in there,
  I will buy ten cakes a week from you."

Rose goes back home.
What can she do?
Nothing has ever stopped Rose.
But now she is stuck.
She can sell her cakes to small shops,
  and get by with no license.
Or she can find a licensed kitchen, and bring her cakes
  to the big time.
But where is there a licensed kitchen?

Wild Rose is on the hunt.
She will find a licensed kitchen!
She will bring her cakes to the big time.
She will go to all the places where she has sold her cakes.
She will ask if she can rent the kitchen.

The Trinidad Shop says yes!
Now, in the morning, Rose goes to the Trinidad Shop.
She spends a long time there.
She bakes from 6 AM until 11 AM.
She makes a big pile of cakes.
After lunch, she boxes up the cakes, and takes them to every end
    of the city.

Rose has made it.
Her cakes are in the big time.
She has cash, and she even has some fame!
She likes to listen to people as they taste her cakes.
She loves it when they rave about her cakes.
"All I want is a taste of those Black Cakes by Rose," says a man.
Rose just smiles.
She smiles a lot these days.

James

Chapter One

This is James.

James is from Senegal.

James began helping his mom at her
food stand in the market when he
was still a kid.

As it happened, James was good
at selling.

"People like James," said his mom.

"They trust him, and they want to buy from him."

Soon James was in the market every day.

He did not go to school.

He could sell so much in the market.

His mom said, "We need you here."

So he went every day.

"How are you so good at selling?" his sister asked him.

James shrugged with a smile. "I just like people," he said.

One day, a man came to his mom.

He was dressed all fine, like a man from the city.

He had been watching James.

"This kid has talent," he said.

"I have a business in Rome.

He can make much more money in the big city."

The man's name was Dave.
He was not a bad man.
He was not a *good* man, but he was not bad.
He just wanted to make money.
He could have been a very bad man, but James was in luck.
James went with Dave.
James was 15.

This is what Dave did:
He would take young men from their small homes in Senegal.
He had fake papers to get them into Rome.
All the boys could share the space in a small home.
Every day they went out and sold things.
Dave had fake papers for all of them.

In Rome, James was still good at selling.
He could sell anything.
He would ask people to help him learn Italian.
Soon he could speak a bit of Italian.
This made him even better at selling.
Dave was watching.

One day Dave came to James.
"James," he said, "I want to send you to another city."
At first James thought this was a punishment.
"Did I do a bad job?" he asked.
"No, no," said Dave. "Not at all.
It is because you are so good."

"OK," said James. "Where are you sending me?"
"I am sending you to the most fantastic city.
I am sending you to Paris.
You will take the top role.
You will be my second in command.
You will be the boss, James."
James was 19.

Chapter Two

James went to Paris.
At first Paris was a big maze that he could not figure out.
But then, just like in Rome, he adapted.
He learned French.
He came to love the French way of life.
He did well as the boss of ten others.

The boys would arrive, scared, from their African home.
James could remember when he felt that way.
He told the boys how to do well.
He made them learn some French words.
The boys felt grateful to James.
They did a good job in the market.

James could have kept his job in Paris for a long time.
Maybe he would have gotten his French citizenship.
Maybe he would have been a happy Frenchman.
But something happened to change everything:
James fell in love!

Clare was a student from New York City.
She loved the things that James and the boys were selling.
They were African trinkets, all hand-made.
At first, she would stop on her way home from class,
    just to admire the trinkets.
But soon, she was stopping because she loved to chat with James.

They chatted in French.
"I hope to learn English one day," said James.
So Clare began to teach him English.

James was handsome and charming.
When he spoke—in French or in English—
    he still had the sounds of Africa.
"I love the way you talk," said Clare.

Soon, Clare and James were running all over the city.
They drank coffee in small shops.

They would explore markets on the far side of the city.
They jumped on the train and explored the small towns.
They visited all the spots in the city that were of note.
They kissed here and there and everywhere in the city.
This was the best time of James' life. He had never felt so happy.

At the end of June, Clare came to James.
"James," she said, "I love you so much!
But I must go back to the US.
My classes here in Paris are finished.
I have one more month here, and then I go back."
James had forgotten that Clare would go back the US.
"But . . . but . . . but . . . You cannot go back!"
Clare gave him a sad smile and a hug.
"I have to go back," she said.

The next month passed too fast.
Soon it was time for Clare to pack her bags.
James drove with her to the airport.
He kissed her and hugged her, and watched her get in line.
He waved and waved until she was gone.
After Clare left, the city was dark and sad. All happiness was gone.
After six months of sadness, James made up his mind.
It was time for him to go.

Chapter Three

James is in the US!
He is living with a friend, Shane.
James's old boss, Dave, has no jobs in the US.
So he is on his own.
But from all his time selling trinkets in Rome and Paris,
    James has many friends all over the globe.
One of them is Shane.
When James asked Shane if he could
    crash at his place on Pine Street,
    Shane said, "Dude! Yes!"

James knows a bit of English, but he
    must have more.
He takes an English class.
It is the first time he has been in a
    class in more than 15 years.
He loves it.

"So?" says Shane. "Did you find that girl yet? What's her name?"
James is prepping for an English test.
"What girl?" he says.
"Oh man! 'What girl?' You forgot your girl that quick?"
"Clare?" says James.
"No, Shane, I did not forget Clare! But I cannot find her until I am
    all set up in the US.
If I go to her now, she would have to take care of me.
I will go to her when I can speak English, and I have a job."

Months go by.

Still James has not called Clare.

"My English is not good yet," he says.

He has a job, though!

He is selling hats and cell phone cases in a mall.

He has lots of friends, and his English is getting better and better.

Now James makes enough cash that at last he can share the cost
     of the rent.

He finds that almost all of his cash goes to Shane for rent.

"Wow, rent is a lot in New York City!" he says.

In Rome and Paris, his boss Dave took care of the rent.

Dave took care of everything.

James did not think about rent or bills.

Now James has to help with all of this.

I am just getting to be an adult now, he thinks.

He is glad to make this change.

In his English class, his teacher tells him he should finish
     high school.

James has never considered finishing high school.

But now he wants to.

He will finish high school, and THEN he will call Clare.

"James! Call Clare!"

Shane thinks James is just stalling.

"Dude! You are just scared! Call her!

You came here to find her.

It has been nine months.

Your English is fine! You have a job.

Stop acting scared! Call her!"
And so, at last, James calls Clare.

"JAMES! Is it really you?"
"Yes! It is me! And I am in New York City!
I came to find you! Because I love you, Clare.
And I miss you."
At last he has said what is in his heart.
On the other end of the line, *nothing*.
Clare says nothing.

Chapter Four

When Shane gets home, he finds James very depressed.
"Dude! Did you call her? What happened?"
James cannot say a thing.

"Dude, just tell me. I can take it. What happened?"
James takes a big breath.
"She . . . she . . . she said I should come meet her husband."

"Oh, dude. Oh, man. Oh dude. You got had."
Shane shakes his head with sadness.
James is flat on the bed.
"Oh man. So sorry! But listen. Listen, dude.
This has been happening since the beginning of time."
Shane shrugs.
"It happens, dude.
Happens on both sides. Man and woman."

It takes James a long time to get over Clare.
She broke his heart.
She was his first love.
And everything he has done in the US has been for her.
Now, it is difficult for him to remember why he should do anything.

Get a better job?
Finish high school?
Get better at English?
Get an apartment for himself?
Why is he doing anything, if not for Clare?
He is sad and despondent.

A month passes.
James begins to wake up from his sadness.
He begins to work hard again, at English and at his job.

At last he begins to think of new plans.
"You know what?" he says to Shane.
"I think I want to have my own stall in the mall.
I want it to be mine. I want to be the boss.
But love? No, not for me.
Never again."

It is spring. James sits on the stoop, watching the people go by.
He has many friends on Pine Street, but he is not there to chat.
He is thinking, and planning his next step.
He is not sure how to start a business.
All of sudden, he sees a woman from his street.
He has seen her, but never met her.
She is the woman who makes the cakes.
She is getting into her van.

"Hello! Hello there, friend. I am James."
Rose smiles at this handsome man. "Hello, James."
"I want to tell you—I like your van! And your cakes are fantastic!"
"Thank you," smiles Rose.
"I want to ask you about your cake business.
Because I want to start a business.
And I am thinking, maybe this lady can advise me."
Rose smiles even more.
"I am in a rush now," she says.
"But I would love to share what I know with you."
She hands him her card. "Call me."
As he watches Rose drive away, James is full of hope.
Maybe it is not so bad here in New York City.

June

Chapter One

This is June.
She is Rose's sister.
June has been living in the US for six years.
When she came here, she left her kids back home.
June's kids are 10 and 12.
They are with June's mom.
June's mom takes good care of the kids.
But June misses them so much.

Now Rose is here with June.
"It's so good be back with my sis," says June.
"I miss my family so much. I miss my kids."
Rose says, "Well, June, I think it's time for you
    to get your kids here."
"No," says June. "I am at the job all the time.
How would I find time to take care of the girls?
They would be left alone too much."

Rose is quick to get mad.
"When you left the girls six years ago," she says, "you told them
    you would send for them.
When I left one year ago, I told them the same thing.

We *must* send for them.
I can help take care of them."

June is resistant.
"I have seen sad cases," she says.
"The moms and dads don't have time for the kids.
The kids don't do well in class.
They waste time on the street.
They drop out of school.
The girls get pregnant. The boys do drugs."

June shakes her head.
"Rose, I have seen this happen to good kids.
It is different here than at home."
But Rose has seen the girls back home.
She knows how much they miss their mom.
She knows their school back home is not good.
She does not want to make June feel bad, but she is not giving up.

Rose takes a big breath.
"June, what can I do to make this happen?
We must bring those girls here.
Here they will have good schools.
They will learn English.
They can get the things that we did not get,
    because we came here too late in life."

June is getting mad.
"Who will pick them up from school?" she says.

"Who will make sure they do their homework?
Who will go to the school to talk to the teachers?
My English is not that good.
And this house is not big.
They will get here expecting a big house."
June starts to sob.
"I wanted to make things perfect before I sent for them."

"Oh!" says Rose. "That is the problem.
June, they just want to be with their mom.
They will not care that things are not perfect."
She hugs June. "You are their mom! It is you they want!"
June nods. "Yes. You are right. Let's do it. Let's send for them!"

Chapter Two

June and Rose are all set to send for the girls.
But first, there are a lot of tasks to take care of.
June goes to the Embassy to find out what she must do.
June is a Legal Permanent Resident.
She is allowed to send for her children.

The lady at the Embassy tells her she should file the application
    on-line.
June is not good with a computer.
But she is willing to take a class.
She takes a one-day class at the library.
When she finishes the class, she files the application on-line.

Rose cannot get over this.
"June, you just took one class, and
    now you can use a computer?"
"It's not that difficult," says June.
"And now I can check on-line to see
    how the application is going."
"The application is complete?" asks Rose. "Just like that?"
"Yes," says June. "It should take about six months
    to get approved."

Now June and Rose must get ready for the girls.
Rose visits the school.
She asks how to enroll the girls.
She meets the English teacher.
She looks over the books and the classroom.

At home, Rose says, "June, I think the school will be good.
There are too many kids in the classroom.
But the English teacher is strict.
The kids listen to her.
They respect her."
June is glad.

But where will the girls sleep?
There are just two bedrooms in the apartment.
"We can hang a blanket in the living room," says Rose.
"They will have a room on this side of the blanket.
This will be fine!"
Rose always thinks things like this are no problem.
June is not so sure.

School, check. Bedrooms, check. What more must they do?
"Clothes!" yells Rose.
"They must have new things!"
June and Rose almost run to the mall.
This part is fun.

Everything is all set.
They just need the application to be finished.
They just need to wait.
June is scared. But filled with hope.

Chapter Three

At last the girls are on their way!
June and Rose are so glad.
So much time has passed.
At last the girls will be here soon.

The girls' names are Hope and Jade.
Hope is 13. She does not smile much.
She looks like she has not made up her mind yet
    about this whole "go-to-America" plan.
Jade is 11. She is full of smiles and fun.
She likes to make people smile back.

"Hello, girls! It's your Auntie Rose!"
Rose grabs the girls in a big hug, and holds them close.
"Oh, my big girls! I missed you so!"

They hug her back.
Even Hope has a big smile to be with her beautiful, fun, loving
    Auntie Rose.

Then it is time to say hello to their mom.
The girls have not seen June in six years.
All of a sudden, there are no smiles.
Everyone is shy.
They all hang back.

"Well. Hello, my girls," says June at last.
She kisses both girls.
They kiss her back.
It is as if they have never met.

It is time to go home.
Rose gets a cab, and they all pile in.
The girls have just two small bags each.
They stare out the window at New York City.

At home, the girls find their small
    room, with a blanket for a wall.
The apartment is small and dark.
The girls look sad.
"Look, girls!" says Rose.
    "We got you gifts!"
The girls smile and run to the pile
    of gifts.

"Do they fit? Do you like them?"
They do fit. And they do like them.

That night, June and Rose take the girls out for dinner.
Rose holds up her glass. "To all of us," she says.
"We will be a family. We will have fun.
We will love and support each other."
June holds up her glass. "You will go to school," she says.
"You will work hard. You will have things we could not have."
The girls nod. They hold up their glasses.
"To all of us," they say.

Chapter Four

It is not easy.
First, the girls must start school.
They do not speak English, just French.
The school has an ESL class.
The girls are in the class one time every day.
The rest of the day they take the regular classes.

At first they understand nothing.
But then, the English comes.
At home they watch TV in English.
They take home extra work from the ESL class.

For Jade, the English comes fast.
She is still small. She can take in new things.

Jade is like Rose.
Life is like a game for her.
She is quick and fast.
She is full of smiles, even when she falls.

For Hope, it is more difficult.
She hates that she is the new kid
    in the class.
She hates that her English
    is not good.
She hates how hard it is to be here.

There is a kid in her ESL class named Fidel.
He is from the Dominican Republic.
She can see in his eyes that he feels the same as her.
It tires you out to be in this new life.
Everything hard. Everything different.

Hope and Fidel are hanging out all the time.
June is upset about this.
"We did not bring her here so she can get a boyfriend!"
Rose says, "Yes, but come here and listen!"
Hope and Fidel are sitting on the front stoop, chatting in English.

Soon, Hope is finished with the ESL class.
She has left Fidel behind.
Hope and Jade are doing well in school.
June thanks God for their good luck.
It is all good.

"What are you thinking about?" June asks Rose.

Rose is sitting by the window. She stares out at the street.

"Just tell me. Everything is fine. Your cake business, my job,
    the girls. It is all good. So why do you look sad?"

"Well . . ." says Rose.

"Yes?" says June.

"I was just thinking . . ."

"Yes?"

"That it's time we bring Mama here!"

June just smiles and shakes her head.

Mike

Chapter One

This is Mike.
Mike is from New York City.
Mike quit school a long time ago.

When Mike was a kid, his dad was a drunk.
He lost his job and never got another job.
He just drank. And yelled. And felt sorry for himself.
When Mike was 12, his mom left his dad.

Mike swore to himself that he would not be like his dad.
"I will not drink," he said.
"I will not sit at home with no plans.
I will not yell at my wife and kids."

But by the time Mike was 16, he was drinking.
By the time he was 19, he was a drunk.
He had quit school.
He had quit everything.

Mike had a job as a line cook in a diner.
He would come to the job hung-over.

He did his time on the job,
and then he went home and got drunk.

Mike had a girlfriend, Eve.
Eve was used to Mike being drunk.
She did not like it, but there was nothing she could do about it.
He was mad a lot, as well.
And there was nothing she could do about this.

One day, Mike's mom came to see him.
"Mike, I have a some bad news," she said.
"I have a problem with my health.
I have breast cancer."

All Mike could do was to just stare back at his mom.
How could she do this to him?
She was all he had left.
That night, Mike went out and got very drunk.

Chapter Two

Mike was no help to his mom.
Eve tried to talk to him.
"I don't want to scare you, Mike, but your mom could die.
You have to help her."

Mike could not listen to this.
If his Mom was not there for him, what
      would happen?
He felt like his world was falling apart.
He was drinking more than ever.

Mike's mom called.
"Mike," she said, "I begin chemo next week.
They will inject drugs into my arm.
It will hurt a lot, and I will be very sick and tired.
Can you help me?
I will need you to bring me home from the hospital."

Mike could not refuse this direct request.
The next week, he came to drive his mom to the hospital.
He came late.
His shirt was untucked.
He did not shave.
And he smelled like wine.

There was not much Mike's mom could do.
"Thank you for coming, Mike," she said.
She sat in the car and did not say anything.
Mike felt sick, and he was mad.
The rage rose up inside of him.

In the hospital, Mike had to run to the bathroom to be sick.
When he came out, his mom had been called in.

He sat and waited.
He could not believe this was happening to him.

First he has a drunk dad.
Then his dad splits.
Now his mom is sick and could die.
What a terrible life he had.
He felt like he had been ripped off.
He felt the rage rise up in him again.

"What kind of cancer do you have?"
A small child asks him this. She is bald and thin.
"What? Oh, no, I don't have cancer," Mike says.
"Oh. You look so sad. I thought you were sick."
"No. No, I'm not sick," says Mike.
Mike spends the next hour waiting for his mom, and thinking.

Chapter Three

Mike is helping his mom.
He takes her to the hospital every week.
He goes to the store for her, and brings her all the foods
    she can still eat.
He makes the food for her.

She just likes junk food.
The chemo makes her sick, and the junk food is all she wants.

She is getting thin.
She has lost most of her hair.

Sometimes, Mike just sits with her.
They watch TV.
Mike is restless, but he sits.
He drinks a six-pack of beer while he sits with her.

One day, Mike's mom has some
    gossip.
"Your dad called me," she says.
"What?!" Mike is shocked.
"He is still alive?"
"Yes," says his mom.
"He has a new wife.
He quit drinking."

"Oh how *wonderful*," says Mike.
"That's so fantastic. What a terrific man.
He messes up your life; he makes my life a complete disaster.
Then he starts all over.
Well, I wish him the best of luck."
Mike pops open another beer and chugs it.

"Mike, how long are you going to punish your dad
    by dragging yourself through the mud?"
"What? What the hell do you mean?"
Mike is all fired up.

"I think you are getting back at him," says his mom,
    "and maybe me, too.
You are committed to messing up your life.
With the drinking, and all the rage you are holding on to."

"WHAT?"
Mike's rage wells up in him like a monster.
"Mom, I HATE that man.
He is the one who messed up my life, not me.
And, in case you didn't notice, he messed up your life, too!!"

Mike runs out of his mom's home.
He runs home.
He crashes around, smashing things and yelling.
Then he falls onto his bed, sobbing, and yelling.
And then, at last, he sleeps.

Chapter Four

It is one year later.
Mike's mom got past the cancer.
She is cancer-free!
Mike helped her through the entire sickness.
He was not always the best at giving care, but he was there.

Then, this is what happened to Mike:
He quit drinking.
That was the biggest thing.

He just stopped . . . and then he started.
And then he stopped again. And started again.
He did that a bunch of times, and at last he stopped for good.

But the rage was still with him, a monster ready to strike
    at any time.
When his mom was all better, he took a trip.
He had no plan.
He just wanted to *go*.
He stuck out his thumb and hitched a ride.
He said, "I will hitch-hike as far as I can go."

Mike hitched rides all across the country.
He made it to the West, to Washington and New Mexico,
    and other states as well.
He picked up jobs when he could.
He slept in the back of trucks and in tunnels and in tents.

After many months of this, he began to miss his home state,
    New York.
He missed his mom. And he missed Eve.
He still felt the rage inside him, but it was smaller.
It was not a monster.
He felt he had chipped away at it.
It was time to go home.

He stuck out his thumb and hitched a ride back home.
A trucker drove him all the way to Delaware.
Another trucker drove him the rest of the way home.

He let him off in the Bronx.
"Thanks, man! I can take the
    subway from here," he said.

Mike went to his mom's home.
"I am still fine, Mike!" she said,
    giving him a big hug.
Mike smiled. "I am better, too,
    Mom.
I am almost fine, too.
Well, I am getting there."

Next, Mike went to Eve's.
"Mike," said Eve. "I am glad you are back home.
But I want some more time before we get back together."
"That's OK," said Mike. "We have time."
He sat on the front stoop with Eve.
"My plan," he said, "is to go back to school.
And then you will see that I am better, and you will see at last
    that I can be a good husband."
"OK, Mike," said Eve, with a brave smile.
"We'll see."

Miles

Chapter One

This is Miles.
Miles is a good kid.
He is a whiz kid at school
    and on the trombone.
He has no siblings.
He is the star in his family.

Miles's mom and dad think that Miles is talented.
They gush about him all the time.
"That is one whiz kid we have," says his dad.
But Miles's mom and dad are at their jobs all the time.
In the summer, Miles helps out at the garden on the next block.
But it is too cold for the garden now.

Miles is alone after school.
He does his homework, and he plays his trombone.
And then he has nothing to do.
Miles's mom frets about this.
"He should have some more pals," she says.
"He is alone too much."

After school, Miles is often bored.
Sometimes, he just stares out the window.
There are interesting things on his street to watch.

The lady with the cakes is always putting her cake boxes in the van.
And a man from Africa is there.
The man who used to live in Paris and Rome.

Miles knows this man, James.
James likes to chat with Miles.
"Hey, my man. How are you today?"
Miles waves to him, and smiles.
And there are two girls.
They are from the same home as the lady with the cakes.
Miles has not chatted with them yet.
But he sees them at school, and here on Pine Street.

One day Miles is sitting at the window.
He stares up and down the street.
Across the street, in the lot, he sees something.
An animal. A small, white animal.
He squints to see better.
It is a dog!

Miles runs outside, and crosses the street to get to the dog.
She has white fur, with a black stripe on her back.
She is shivering, and looks scared.
He can see her ribs.
"You need food and a bath, don't you, girl?"
Miles is all set to help her.
But is she friendly?

Miles squats down and holds out his hand.
"Here, girl. Hello. It's OK."
The dog comes close and sniffs his hand.
She wags her tail.
Then she wags her entire body.

Chapter Two

Miles has a project.
He must get food, water, and shelter for this dog.
He runs back home.
He finds a big box, and fills a dish with water.
He takes cash from the box under his bed.
This is where he hides his cash.

Miles sets up a little home for the dog in the far end of the lot.
She has a box to hide in.
She has a dish of water.
She has a plate with a pile of dog food on it.
She looks content to be in her new home, with Miles there.

"Is that your dog?"
Miles looks up with a gasp.
It's those two girls, the new ones.
They share the home with the lady who makes the cakes.
Uh oh.
Miles stares back at them.
Can he trust them?

"Yes, this is my dog."
"What's its name?" the smaller girl asks.
"It's a she. Not an it," Miles says, acting offended.
"So what's her name?"
"Her name is . . . her name is . . . well, I just call her Little Gal."

"Can I pet her? Will she bite?"
"No, she won't bite. She's a good dog.
She's tame. Just let her sniff you first."
Jade, the small, brave one, holds out her hand.
She lets Little Gal sniff her.
Little Gal wags her tail and licks the girl's hand.

"Why do you make her stay out here?"
The bigger girl, Hope, glares at Miles.
"Uh . . ." Miles can't think fast.
"It's not your dog, is it?"
Miles says nothing, just pets Little Gal.
"So if it's not your dog, then whose dog is it?"
Hope is relentless!

Miles just shrugs and strokes Little Gal's white back.
"Well," says Jade, "she should be your dog.
I can tell you love her."
Miles is grateful to Jade for understanding.
But Hope will not stop.
"No way will your mom and dad let you keep her," she says.
"Yes, they will," says Miles.
"No, they won't."
Miles falls silent.

"We should bathe her!" says Jade.
Miles nods. "Yes! She should get a bath. But where?"
"Not in our home!" says Hope.
The kids hide the dog inside the box and go up to Miles's home.
Hope will not let Jade go into the bathroom.
"Mama will kill you if she finds out we came here.
And in a bathroom with a boy? No!"
So Miles bathes Little Gal by himself, while Hope and Jade
    sit in the living room.
When it is time to take Little Gal back outside, Miles can't do it.

Chapter Three

"I will hide her in here," says Miles.
Jade and Hope stare at him in shock.
"You can't hide a dog from your mom and dad," says Hope.
"Why not? It's not a crime to hide a dog," says Miles.
"Help me get her set up."
The girls cannot resist a project like this.

"I have a closet in my room," says Miles.
"I can hide her in there," he says.

When his mom and dad get home, Miles goes to sit
    in the living room.
He takes care to shut his door.
His mom makes him a quick snack.
"How was your day, Big Man?" she asks.
This is her nickname for Miles.
"It was good," says Miles.
"What happened that was good?"
Miles shrugs. "Nothing much."
But his heart is pumping hard in his chest.

For dinner, Miles's mom makes baked chicken.
She shakes it in crushed crackers to make a crust, and then bakes it.
It is the best chicken. Miles loves this dish.
When no one is looking, Miles takes a bit of chicken in his hand,
    and places it in his pocket.
"Miles!" his father says. "Why are you putting chicken
    in your pocket?"
"Uh . . ." Miles has to think fast. "For a snack.
For when it's late, if I want a snack."
"Miles!" scolds his mom. "Don't put food in your pocket.
You can get a snack in the kitchen if you want one."
"OK," says Miles. He puts the chicken back, but not all of it.

It's bedtime.
Miles kisses his mom and dad goodnight.

When he gets into his room, he shuts the door, and locks the latch.
He takes Little Gal out of the closet.
She is so happy to see him. She wags her tail, and jumps around.
He takes the chicken out of his pocket and hands it to her.
She gulps it down.

Miles is all set for bed, but something is not OK with Little Gal.
She stares at him. She whines. Then she glares at him.
Oh! All of a sudden Miles remembers that she did not go
    to the bathroom.
How could he have forgotten this?
He can't take her out at this time of night!

Miles hatches a plan.
He takes the basket he uses for his dirty clothes.
He attaches a rope to the basket, and then puts Little Gal
    in the basket.
He opens the window.
He lets Little Gal down into the yard.
But will she get back into the basket?

Miles lets the basket down into the yard.
When the basket lands, Little Gal jumps out.
She runs around the yard, sniffing and scratching.
She does her business.
Then she looks up at Miles.
She does not get the plan.
She whines at Miles.

"Get in the basket!" Miles says in a stage-whisper.
He tugs on the rope so the basket jumps a bit.
Little Gal whines. Then she scratches on the basket.
"Get in!"
She jumps in the basket.
Miles is amazed! He is astonished!
He pulls up the basket, and takes Little Gal out of the basket.
Time for a big hug!
She is the best dog!

Chapter Four

"Miles, what is this?" Miles' mom is upset.
She is holding up his pants.
There is a big rip in the pants.
Miles stares. "Uh . . ." He can't think.
"Where did this rip come from?"
"Uh . . . I think I went over a gate.
Yes, that's it.
I went over a gate, and the leg got stuck
    on the gate."
"A gate? What gate?
"Uh, in the lot across the street."
"Oh." Miles's mom is silent.
She does not think of Miles as a kid
    who goes over gates.
He is a shy kid, who just does his homework.
In fact, she often thinks he is alone too much.

It is Saturday. No school.
Miles lets the basket down into the yard,
    with Little Gal inside the basket.
Then he runs outside.
"Where are you going, Miles?!" his dad yells.
"Outside! To hang out with Hope and Jade!"

Miles's mom and Dad exchange glances.
"Who are Hope and Jade?" asks his dad.
"I think they are those girls next door."
"Is he into girls? At his age?"
Miles's mom shrugs.
She thinks something is up with Miles,
    but she does not know what.

Miles and Jade and Hope take Little Gal to the small park
    at the end of Pine Street.
She gets to run around and around.
She jumps up on the bench, and runs all over.
She is wagging her tail and jumping up and down.
It makes them all smile.
Even Hope is giggling.
Little Gal is so happy.
"See?" says Miles. "This is why it's good to have a dog.
She makes us all smile."

Miles tells his mom and dad that he wants to take up jogging.
"I only have time to do it before school," he tells them.
Every morning, Miles wakes up at 6 A.M., and dresses
    in jogging clothes.

But he does not go jogging.
He takes Little Gal to the park.
He lets her run around and do her business.
Then he takes her back home.
He runs back up to his bedroom with her in his arms.
He hands her a plate of food, and puts her in the bed
    he has made for her in the closet.
Then he shuts his bedroom door, and wakes up his mom and dad.
This goes on for two weeks.

"Miles? What is this?"
Miles's mom is holding up a ragged bit of cloth.
"I don't know," says Miles. "What is it?"
"At one time, it was my white jacket. Now it is a rag.
What the heck is happening, Miles?
All these things are rags!
It is like we have a dog in the house!"
Miles just shrugs. "I don't know," he says.

Of course, this cannot go on.
Two weeks is a long time to hide a dog in a small home!
One day, Miles wakes up to find his mom in running clothes.
"Good morning, Miles! I would like to go running with you . . ."
All of a sudden, she yells.
"AHHH! Miles! There is a dog in your closet!

"Miles, what the hell is happening here?"
Miles knows his mom is upset when she uses the H word!
"I am in an extreme state of shock here, Miles.

A dog? You have kept a dog in here? For how long?
Miles, this is insane! How did you do this?"

Now Miles's dad wakes up from the yelling.
"A dog? What the—? Huh? What?"
Miles's mom tells him what is happening.
All of a sudden, Miles's dad explodes—not with yelling,
    but with grinning.

"Miles, you amaze me," he says.
He looks at his wife with a big grin.
"That is some kind of whiz kid we have here."

Miles's dad is so impressed with Miles.
"That he could hide that dog from us?"
He just shakes his head, amazed and impressed.
Miles's mom is not so impressed.
But she likes that Miles has made friends with Hope and Jade,
    and that it was the dog that did it.
She likes that he has a dog pal to be with when he is alone
    after school.
"Miles, we think Little Gal should be your dog for all time."
Miles smiles and hugs Little Gal.

Jane

Chapter One

This is Jane.
For most of her life, Jane has been
    a teacher.
Five years ago, she had to retire.
Jane is the kind of retired person
    who is still full of life.
For these five long years of retirement,
    she has been bored.

Jane likes to move.
She has to stay busy!
She takes a jog in the park every day.
On her way home, she stops in at the Public Garden
    on Aspen Street.
She has become friends with Bethann, the woman
    who made the garden happen.

"I love this place!" she says to Bethann.
"It is such a great place for all the people in this district.
You should be very proud of yourself that you made this happen."
Bethann smiles, but she does not look happy.
"What's the matter?" asks Jane. "Is there a problem?"

"There is always a problem," says Bethann.
"We still have to come up with the funding
    to keep the garden open.
A non-profit came up with most of the cash to keep the lot
    from being developed.
But we still must get the rest of the cash.
And the city will close the garden if we don't get this money!"

"How much is it?" ask Jane.
"We must come up with five thousand dollars," says Bethann.
"Five thousand dollars?!" Jane almost yells.
"Now, what makes them think a little public garden can come up
    with five thousand dollars?"
Bethann shakes her head. "I don't know," she says.
"And I am all tired out from this mess.
Someone else is going to have to take this over."

"That is such a shame," says Jane.
"The city should be ashamed.
They should not close this garden."
She shakes her head in disgust.
She stares at the kids planting things, at the moms resting,
    and at the people chatting.
"They always take things away. Things the public needs."

Jane starts getting mad.
"Bethann, you can't let them do this!
You have to push back," she says.

"Don't let them take away this garden.
You just have to organize the people, and make that money."

"Oh, is that all?" says Bethann.
"Just organize the people," she says, with a tired tone.
"I am telling you, Jane, I am all tired out."
She stares at Jane. "Somebody else has to do it.
Somebody with time on her hands . . ."
"OK, fine!" says Jane at last.
"If nobody else will save this garden, then I will step up."
She smiles at Bethann. "I'll just want a bit of help from you."

Chapter Two

"First things first," says Bethann.
"You have to have a plan."
She and Jane are going to save this garden.
Well, just Jane. Bethann is just getting her set up.
"When you are all set up, I will step back and relax,"
    she says to Jane.
"No more of this planning work
    for me."
Jane just smiles.

"We must have a way to make all
    this cash," says Bethann.
"So let's think on it.
How can we make a lot of money?"

The two women stare at each other with blank faces.
"I know. Let's take it to the garden," says Jane at last.
"We will go to the public to find a plan."

Jane calls a meeting in the garden.
It is springtime, and everyone is glad to be there.
Jane stands up. "Hello, everyone," she says. "My name is Jane.
We are here today because we need a plan to get the money
    to save the garden."
All of sudden, Bethann is there.
"I'll take it from here," she says.
Jane just smiles and steps back.

"You all remember that big meeting last fall?" she says.
"Congressman Smith got us a grant to save the garden.
But we still need to come up with the rest: five thousand dollars.
So we are here today to get your input.
How can we do this?
Where can we get this money?"

"A bake sale!" someone yells.
"Bake sales don't make that much money," says another.
"We could show films in the garden."
"Have a jazz band in the garden. Everyone has to buy a ticket."
"Sell eggs!"
"Have a tag sale!"
"Sell our radishes and squashes!"
Everyone yells out things they can do to make money.

Mel stands up.
"These are good plans," he says.
"But I think we should pick just one thing.
One big thing. We all work on it together.
And we should bring in money from other places.
It can't be our money.
We won't have enough."

Next a woman steps up.
"I am Mrs. Velazquez," she says.
"I am the principal of the public school at the end of Ash Street.
But I am also a resident of Aspen Street.
And I love this garden.
At my school our funding gets cut all the time,
    and we have to find more funds.
I think the same thing as Mel.
We need one big plan."

"Some school districts hold a race," Mrs. Velazquez says.
The public signs up to run or stroll five miles.
It is $20 to enter.
But then people get sponsors.
You find people or stores who will give you money
    for running the race.
It is a good way to get a lot of people invested in your project.
And to get a lot of funds.
I think we should hold a race like this."

Chapter Three

The race is on.
Signs are up all over the district.
"Run Five Miles, or just pay me to run it!"
This is Miles's sign.
Jade's says, "5 Miles to Save the Garden!"
"Sign up!" yell Miles and Jade.

"What would we do without
    those kids?" says Jane.
"I don't think we would have
    this garden," smiles
    Bethann.
"Let's ask them to find more
    people."
Jane calls to Jade and Miles.
"You kids should go to Ash
    Street, and Elm Street,
    and Chestnut Street.
Take lots of signs with you.
    Put the signs up all over."

While they are putting up signs, Jade and Miles cross paths
    with Beth and Rick.
Beth and Rick are holding hands and kissing.
"Ooh, they're in love," says Jade, giggling.
"Yuck!" says Miles. "Disgusting!"
He bends over and pretends to puke.
When Beth and Rick get close, they stand up, still giggling.

Jade tells Beth and Rick what is happening,
    while Miles holds up a sign about the race.
"A race? To save that garden?" Beth is interested.
"Rick, we should do this!" she says.
"Babe, you know I'm in school that day," says Rick.
"And I have a big exam coming up.
But you should go. Take your pal Pam."
"OK, I will!" says Beth.
"And you go do a good job on your exam. You will be a cop soon!"
She adds her name to the list.

Next, Jade and Miles run into two women.
They are jogging, and chatting all the while.
It is Clem and Ying.
Ying's English is so good.
"Help us save the garden!" says Miles.
They tell Clem and Ying about the race.
Clem takes the poster from Miles and reads it to herself.
"I can run five miles!" she says.

"I love pretty things, just like that garden," says Ying.
"I will run the five miles with you, Clem.
And my store will also be a sponsor!"
Clem takes a poster to bring back to her job.
"I think a lot of my pals at work will want to run," she says.
"My job wants us all to get in good shape.
I will ask my boss if he can be a sponsor."

Next Miles and Jade run into a man and woman with two infants.
"Oh! So cute!" says Hope. "And they're twins!

Don't you think they're so cute, Miles?"
Miles smiles and nods.
The mom and dad, Grant and Fran, listen to the kids describe the race.
"Do we have to run?" asks Grant. "Can we just stroll?"
"Grant," says Fran. "We have a jog stroller. We will run."
Grant nods with a tired smile. "Yes, my wife is so wise.
      We can run."

Miles and Hope are finding lots of of people
      who want to run the race.
"Five mile race!" they yell. "Save the garden on Aspen Street!
Aspen Street has a garden. So you don't have to!"
They are getting silly.
But it is working!
They come back to Bethann and Jane with a long list of names.
The list has people who want to race,
      and people who want to sponsor.

Chapter Four

At last, it is time for the race.
Bethann is up front, telling people where to go.
She is yelling and calling and directing everyone.
She comes back to check in with Jane.
"Just going to ask me for a bit of help, hmm?"
      says Bethann to Jane.
"Then I'll get to sit back and relax?"
Jane grins back at her.
"You are good at this," she says.
"I could not have done this without you."

People are milling around at the starting line.
They are attaching numbers to their backs, to their kids,
    and to their strollers.
Jane takes the cash and checks, and puts them into the cash box.
"How are we doing?" asks Miles's dad, as he hands Jane a check.
"Are we going to make it? Five grand?"
"We're getting there," smiles Jane. But she is not so sure.

Rose and James drive by in Rose's big van.
They stop the van.
"We cannot run," says Rose.
"We have to take the cakes all over the city.
But we wanted to check on how it is going!"
James waves at the biggest sign.
"We are with you, Aspen Street Garden!"
The biggest sign says, "Five Mile Race,
    Sponsored by Rose's Black Cakes!"

The girls, Hope and Jade, are there, in their running clothes.
Hope is good at running.
But so is June!
"I will race you," say June.
"I will race you, Mama," says Hope.
Jade says, "I'm going to go with Miles and Little Gal.
We will go at Little Gal's pace. She can't run that fast!"
"I'm glad you have such a good pal," says June.
"I'm glad about that, too!" It is Miles's mom.
She shakes hands with June.
"So glad to meet you at last."

Frank is in line, in his running clothes.
"Just one ticket?" says Jane.
Frank shakes his head. "Two. My wife is on her way.
She just got made Assistant Branch Manager.
At the last second she had to rush in to the job.
She is going to try to get in here in time.
But she has to take care of some things at the bank first."
All of a sudden, Jinx is at his side.
She is in her bank clothes, with running shoes in hand.
"I made it! But I did not have time to change.
Let's just walk the race."
Frank takes her hand, kisses her, and then smiles at Jane.
"Did I tell you my wife is the new Assistant Branch Manager?"

Isabel's mother and Mr. Griffin are getting their numbers.
"It's OK if we just stroll?" asks Isabel's mother.
"I cannot run in these fine clothes.
But I will take a stroll with my elegant husband.
Too bad Isabel is at the job."

"Name, please?"
"We are Mr. and Mrs. Griffin," says Isabel's mother,
      with a big smile.

Jonathan and Lindell are there.
"Jamal! Come on!" yells Jonathan.
"He always has his nose in a book!" he says to Lindell.
He shakes his head, but you can tell he is so proud.
"He loves to sit in the garden and read," Lindell tells Jane
      as she takes her number.
"We are running this race to save the garden for our son."
"Anything to save that garden!" says Jonathan.

All of a sudden Bethann stares, and then gasps.
"I can never forget those glasses," she says.
She shakes hands with Ms. Minton, the lady from City Hall.
"What are you doing here?" Bethann is shocked to see her!
"Well I am running in this race," Ms. Minton says with a smile.
"But you hate our garden," says Bethann.
"I have to admit, Bethann, your work here changed my mind.
Not only did you make a garden where there was nothing,
      but you got all these people together."
"Well, thank you," says Bethann.

"*And* I am here to give you some good news," says Ms. Minton.
"I made some calls. I spoke to the district rep.
He said he will come up with the funds that are still missing.
Anything you don't make in this race, the district rep will
      make up."
Bethann has to grab Ms. Minton and give her a big hug.

"And now," says Ms. Minton, "I think we have a race to run."
And with that, Bethann and Ms. Minton get in line to start the race.

In the end, the garden was saved.
And life went on, all up and down Ash Street, Elm Street,
    Aspen Street, and Pine Street, and everywhere else in the city.